PRESIDENTIAL
CHALLENGE

PRESIDENTIAL CHALLENGE

A Multiple Choice Journey Through
the Twists and Turns
of Our Presidential Elections

★ 1789 to 2004 ★

MARILYN ZUPNIK

DLM Books
Excelsior, Minnesota
2005

DLM Books
Excelsior, Minnesota

Published by DLM Books
P.O. Box 72, Excelsior, MN 55331

Printed by Denison Companies, Bloomington, Minnesota

Cover design graphics by Mary Christopherson

Cover photo campaign buttons courtesy of the collection of
Paul Bengston, Eden Prairie, Minnesota

Library of Congress Control Number 2004116463

ISBN 0-9763773-0-6

www.presidential-challenge.com

Printed in the United States of America

ACKNOWLEDGMENTS

I would like to thank Nancy Meyer of WeMentor, Inc., Minneapolis, for her advice and expertise in the preparation of this book.

I would also like to thank Paul Bengston for permission to photograph campaign buttons from his wonderful collection of campaign memorabilia.

Front cover campaign buttons, from the top clockwise:

William Jennings Bryan/Adlai Stevenson, 1900
William Howard Taft, 1908
William McKinley, 1900
William McKinley/Theodore Roosevelt, 1900
Alton B. Parker/Henry G. Davis, 1904
Theodore Roosevelt, 1904
William Jennings Bryan and Lady Liberty, 1908
Center: Theodore Roosevelt, 1904

For Lea and Dan

and my Mother and Father and Jill

With thanks for your encouragement and support

★ ★ ★ ★ ★

Every four years, the people of the United States choose a leader. We have a grand old time: cheering conventions, smiling candidates, parades, rallies, promises, speeches, and, of course, lots of $$$!

We go to the polls and the President is chosen – not directly by the popular vote, but by the vote of the Electoral College.

What is the Electoral College? How much do you know about our system of deciding on a President, and how much do you know about our Presidential election history?

Read the question, turn the page for the answer!

TEST YOUR KNOWLEDGE!!!

★ ★ ★ ★ ★

CONTENTS

FOREWORD

The history of our presidential elections includes great triumphs and crushing defeats. Candidates have come and gone, parties have been in and out of power, but our system of choosing a chief executive has survived it all.

Democrat, Republican, Liberal and Conservative, people haven't changed; they're about the same as they've always been. If you think the campaigns of today are overly partisan, read about the accusations hurled by supporters of John Adams and Thomas Jefferson in 1796, or how Abraham Lincoln was attacked in the press when he ran for President.

You may be surprised!

❧ General Knowledge ❧

★ *GENERAL KNOWLEDGE* ★ *QUESTIONS* ★

1. If you want to be President of the United States, you must be at least:

> **a.** 25 years old.   **b.** 30 years old.
> **c.** 35 years old.   **d.** 40 years old.

★   ★   ★

2. Which document describes how we elect the President?

> **a.** The Declaration of Independence   **b.** The Bill of Rights
> **c.** The Statute of Voting   **d.** The Constitution

★   ★   ★

3. Why do we vote in November?

a. November had always been a slow month for business, and the merchants had time to travel to the polls then.

b. The farmers needed time for the harvest before they could take time to travel to the polls.

c. November was picked at random.

d. To keep the campaign season as long as possible

★   ★   ★

4. Why do we vote on the Tuesday after the first Monday in November?

a. Lawmakers didn't want voting day to fall on November 1st.

b. The first Tuesday of a month was traditionally reserved for taking inventory in businesses.

c. Monday was considered unlucky.

d. The first Tuesday in November was originally reserved for Thanksgiving.

1. c. 35 years old. You must also be a natural born American citizen and have been a resident in the U.S. for at least 14 years. To become Vice-President, you must meet the same qualifications.

★ ★ ★

2. d. The Constitution. Article II, Section I describes how the President is to be elected.

★ ★ ★

3. b. The farmers needed time for the harvest before they could take time to travel to the polls. The U.S. was largely a farming society at first, and much of the population needed time for the harvest in the fall. For those who attended church on Sundays, Tuesday was a good day for voting, as many needed an extra day to travel to the polls.[1] Many polling places were located at the county seat - a trip of some distance for many voters which could take considerably longer than it does today!

★ ★ ★

4. a. Lawmakers didn't want voting day to fall on November 1st. November 1st was a holiday for many: All Saints Day. In addition, many businessmen reserved the first of the month for doing their books, and Congress felt that the economic gains or losses of the preceding month might influence votes.

For 50 years, Congress permitted the states to vote on any day within a 34 day period before the Electoral College met in December. However, with this arrangement, states voting later could be influenced by the results of those that voted earlier, as in 1832 when Rhode Island voted on Wednesday, November 21st, but its newspaper of November 17th had an article entitled "Election of President" with election results from states that had already voted![2]

A uniform voting day for all the states became necessary. In 1845, the Tuesday after the first Monday in November - in years divisible by four - was established as the voting date for Presidential elections.[3]

★ *GENERAL KNOWLEDGE* ★ *QUESTIONS* ★

5. Which President was elected more times than anyone else?

    a. Thomas Jefferson   **b.** Abraham Lincoln
    c. Ulysses S. Grant   **d.** Franklin D. Roosevelt

★ ★ ★

6. Besides George H. W. Bush and George W. Bush, which of the following were father and son and were both elected President?

    a. John Adams and John Quincy Adams
    b. William Henry Harrison and Benjamin Harrison
    c. Andrew Johnson and Lyndon Johnson
    d. Theodore Roosevelt and Franklin D. Roosevelt

★ ★ ★

7. Which of the following were grandfather and grandson and were both elected President?

    a. James Madison and Zachary Taylor
    b. William Henry Harrison and Benjamin Harrison
    c. Andrew Johnson and Lyndon Johnson
    d. Theodore Roosevelt and Franklin D. Roosevelt

★ ★ ★

8. Which President was elected to two non-consecutive terms?

    a. James Monroe   **b.** Andrew Jackson
    c. Grover Cleveland   **d.** Woodrow Wilson

5. **d. Franklin D. Roosevelt.** He was elected four times: in 1932, 1936, 1940 and 1944. Roosevelt was the only President to be elected to more than two terms.

★ ★ ★

6. **a. John Adams (1797-1801) and John Quincy Adams (1825-1829.)** John Adams was our 2nd President; his son, John Quincy Adams, was our 6th President.

★ ★ ★

7. **b. William Henry Harrison (1841) and Benjamin Harrison (1889-1893).** James Madison and Zachary Taylor were second cousins; Theodore Roosevelt and Franklin D. Roosevelt were fifth cousins; Andrew Johnson and Lyndon Johnson were not related. Research by genealogists has shown that Franklin D. Roosevelt was related either by blood or marriage to eleven other Presidents: George Washington, John Adams, John Quincy Adams, James Madison, Martin van Buren, William Henry Harrison, Zachary Taylor, Ulysses S. Grant, Benjamin Harrison, William Howard Taft and Theodore Roosevelt.[4]

★ ★ ★

8. **c. Grover Cleveland.** **(1885-1889 and 1893-1897)** Cleveland served one term, lost to Benjamin Harrison in the election of 1888, and came back to defeat Harrison four years later.

9. **What is a party caucus?**

    a. A meeting of candidates
    b. A meeting of members of different political parties
    c. A meeting of members of the same political party to nominate candidates for office
    d. A party for members of a political party

★ ★ ★

10. **What is a party platform?**

    a. The candidates nominated by a party for President and Vice-President
    b. The issues favored by a political party, usually during an election campaign
    c. The building that hosts a political convention
    d. The stage from which speeches are given at a political convention

★ ★ ★

11. **How were Presidential candidates chosen in our early elections?**

    a. By Congressional caucus   **b.** By state legislatures
    c. By popular vote   **d.** By state parties

★ ★ ★

12. **How are Presidential candidates chosen today?**

    a. By Congressional caucus
    b. By state legislatures
    c. By statewide party caucuses, primary elections and national conventions
    d. By state parties

9. c. **A meeting of members of the same political party to nominate candidates for office.**

★ ★ ★

10. b. **The issues favored by a political party, usually during an election campaign.** The first party platform appeared at the Democratic convention of 1836.

★ ★ ★

11. a. **By Congressional caucus.** Members of each party in Congress would meet to decide on the nominee. Presidential candidates were chosen by Congressional caucus from 1796 to 1824. This was ironic, as the founding fathers had opposed granting Congress the authority to choose the Chief Executive, for fear that he would be beholden to Congress.

★ ★ ★

12. c. **By statewide party caucuses, primary elections and national conventions.** Most political parties hold national conventions today to officially nominate their presidential candidates. Delegates to the conventions are selected by statewide party caucuses (where voting is done without secret ballots) or in state primary elections. And some delegates to the national conventions are chosen for their political prominence in the party.

13. In which election did Presidential primaries first come into widespread use?

      a. 1896   **b.** 1912   **c.** 1920   **d.** 1928

★ ★ ★

14. Which state traditionally holds the first Presidential primary?

      a. Iowa   **b.** South Carolina
      c. New Hampshire   **d.** Ohio

★ ★ ★

15. Since 1988, several states have held their primaries on the same day in March. This day is known as:

      a. Primary Tuesday.   **b.** Super Tuesday.
      c. Presidential Tuesday.   **d.** Crazy Tuesday.

★ ★ ★

16. What is a PAC?
      a. A candidate's fundraising staff
      b. An advisory panel to a candidate
      c. An independent special interest group that raises
           money for candidates it favors
      d. A pretty active committee

13. b. 1912. In the late 1800's, political party bosses controlled the selection of candidates. Several states held primaries in 1912. However, at that time, the candidate who won the most number of delegates at the primary did not necessarily win the nomination, as delegates' votes were bartered and brokered by party bosses at state and national conventions. This has gradually changed; since the 1970's, candidates who have won the most delegates in the primaries have gone on to win the nomination, thus shifting control of the nominating process to the voters.   ★   ★   ★

14. c. New Hampshire. New Hampshire's first official primary was held in March, 1916; it was scheduled to coincide with Town Meeting Day so they wouldn't have to light up the Town Hall twice! Indiana voted a week earlier and Minnesota voted on the same day as New Hampshire that year. Four years later, Indiana had changed its day to May and Minnesota had discontinued its primary. Since then, New Hampshire has remained No. 1 on the primary schedule. In 1977, New Hampshire passed a law that "eliminates any possible future encroachment on the state's being first."[5] Iowa holds its caucus earlier, but no other primary is held before New Hampshire's.

★   ★   ★

15. b. Super Tuesday. The term "Super Tuesday" was first used in 1988 when nine southern states held their primaries on Tuesday, March 8th. Democrats in these states decided to hold a "regional" primary, hoping to influence the selection of a moderate candidate that would be sympathetic to Southern issues. The list of states participating in Super Tuesday has varied somewhat since then, but candidates who have emerged victorious on those days have usually gone on to win the nomination of their party.[6] On March 7, 2000 there were eleven primaries, a new "Super Tuesday," or "Titanic Tuesday."[7]

★   ★   ★

16. c. An independent special interest group that raises money for candidates it favors. PAC stands for "Political Action Committee."

17. What does the McCain-Feingold Law affect?

        a. The voting age
        b. The length of campaigns
        c. Campaign contributions and advertising
        d. Primary election laws

★   ★   ★

18. In what year did we begin counting the popular vote in Presidential elections?

    a. 1824   **b.** 1832   **c.** 1840   **d.** 1860

★   ★   ★

19. Which election had the highest percentage of voter turnout?

    a. 1860   **b.** 1876   **c.** 1916   **d.** 1944

★   ★   ★

20. What was the main requirement for a citizen to be eligible to vote in our early Presidential elections?

    a. Earning enough money   **b.** Owning property
    c. Having served in the military   **d.** Having a family

17. c. Campaign contributions and advertising. Sponsored by Republican Senator John McCain of Arizona and Democratic Senator Russ Feingold of Wisconsin, the McCain-Feingold Campaign Finance Law limits political fundraising and advertising. It was passed in 2002, and is also known as the Bipartisan Campaign Reform Act of 2002.

★ ★ ★

18. a. 1824. Approximately 350,000 votes were cast for President in 1824.

★ ★ ★

19. b. 1876. The turnout in 1876 was 81.8% of eligible voters. The second highest turnout was in 1860, with 81.2% of eligible voters going to the polls. The voting age public includes all persons over the age of 18 as reported by the Census Bureau. Approximately 7-10% of the adult population (non-citizens and felons) are not eligible to vote.

★ ★ ★

20. b. Owning property. White male "freeholders," or those who held an estate of land through inheritance, were the first Americans allowed to vote. Some states eased this restriction earlier than others; states like Virginia that retained their freeholder requirements longer than others were not able to attract new residents. Other voting requirements included extended residence in a state, being a taxpayer, being able to read, and being the father of a family. With the election of Andrew Jackson in 1828, there arose a greater awareness regarding voting restrictions, which eventually led to significant changes in voter qualifications.

21. The 22nd Amendment to the Constitution:

    a. limits the President to two terms.
    b. sets new campaign fundraising laws.
    c. affects primary elections.
    d. changed voting procedures.

★   ★   ★

22. Who was the youngest candidate to be elected President?

    a. Thomas Jefferson   **b.** Theodore Roosevelt
    c. John F. Kennedy   **d.** Bill Clinton

★   ★   ★

23. Who was the oldest candidate to be elected?

    a. George Washington   **b.** William Henry Harrison
    c. Zachary Taylor   **d.** Ronald Reagan

★   ★   ★

24. Who was the youngest major party Presidential candidate?

    a. Henry Clay   **b.** Stephen Douglas
    c. William Jennings Bryan   **d.** Thomas E. Dewey

21. **a. limits the President to two terms.** Ratified in 1951, the 22nd Amendment to the Constitution limits the President to two terms. According to the Twenty-second Amendment: "No person shall be elected to the office of the President more than twice, and no person who has held the office of President, or acted as President, for more than two years of a term to which some other person was elected President shall be elected to the office of President more than once."

★ ★ ★

22. **c. John F. Kennedy.** At 43, Kennedy was the youngest person to be elected President. Vice-President Theodore Roosevelt became President at 42, upon the assassination of William McKinley.

★ ★ ★

23. **d. Ronald Reagan.** Reagan was elected to the Presidency at the age of 69 in 1980, and at 73 in 1984.

★ ★ ★

24. **c. William Jennings Bryan.** Bryan was 36 when he ran as the Democratic candidate for President in 1896.

25. What city has hosted the most national conventions?

      a. New York   **b.** Boston
      c. Philadelphia   **d.** Chicago

★ ★ ★

26. How many Vice-Presidents have been elected President?

     a. 5   **b.** 9   **c.** 12   **d.** 15

★ ★ ★

27. Who was the first incumbent President to actively campaign for reelection?

      a. Theodore Roosevelt   **b.** William Howard Taft
      c. Woodrow Wilson   **d.** Franklin D. Roosevelt

★ ★ ★

28. Which candidate ran unsuccessfully as the Democratic nominee for President three times?

      a. Franklin Pierce   **b.** Samuel J. Tilden
      c. William Jennings Bryan   **d.** Adlai Stevenson

25. **d. Chicago.**

★ ★ ★

26. **b. 9.** John Adams, Thomas Jefferson, Martin van Buren, Theodore Roosevelt, Calvin Coolidge, Harry Truman, Lyndon Johnson, Richard Nixon and George H. W. Bush.

Adams, Jefferson, van Buren, Nixon and Bush completed their terms as Vice-President and went on to win election to the Presidency. Theodore Roosevelt, Coolidge, Truman and Johnson succeeded to the Presidency upon the death of their predecessors and were then elected to a term as President. Four Vice-Presidents who became President upon the death of their predecessor – John Tyler, Millard Fillmore, Andrew Johnson and Chester A. Arthur – were not subsequently elected President. Gerald Ford, who became President upon the resignation of Richard Nixon, was not elected President.

Declared John Adams, our first Vice-President: "My country has in its wisdom contrived for me the most insignificant office that ever the intention of man contrived or his imagination conceived."

★ ★ ★

27. **b. William Howard Taft.** In 1912, Taft went out on the campaign trail, breaking the tradition of Presidents before him.

★ ★ ★

28. **c. William Jennings Bryan.** The Democrats nominated Bryan in 1896, 1900 and 1908. He never won. In 1912, with three major candidates running, Democrat Woodrow Wilson was elected with fewer popular votes than Bryan received in any of his three tries for the Presidency.

29. Who was the first "dark horse" Presidential candidate?

    a. James K. Polk   **b.** Zachary Taylor
    c. Franklin Pierce   **d.** Abraham Lincoln

★ ★ ★

30. Which Presidential candidate made an appearance during a campaign playing the saxophone?

    a. Warren G. Harding   **b.** Calvin Coolidge
    c. Jimmy Carter   **d.** Bill Clinton

★ ★ ★

31. In what year was the first wartime Presidential election?

    a. 1808   **b.** 1812   **c.** 1848   **d.** 1864

★ ★ ★

32. In what year were secret ballots first used?

    a. 1789   **b.** 1832   **c.** 1860   **d.** 1888

29. a. James K. Polk. A "dark horse" candidate is someone who is believed unlikely to win nomination or election, but is chosen – often as a compromise – when more well-known candidates cannot be agreed upon by party leaders. The term "dark horse," which originally referred to a race horse that was unknown or whose qualities were concealed, made its way into the English language in the early 1800's.

★　★　★

30. d. Bill Clinton. A talented saxophone player since his high school days, Bill Clinton appeared on the Arsenio Hall show during the 1992 campaign. Other Presidents who have been musicians include: Thomas Jefferson, violin, clavichord and cello; John Quincy Adams, flute; Chester Arthur, banjo; Woodrow Wilson, violin; Harry Truman, piano; and Richard Nixon, piano and accordion. Warren G. Harding was known to have played the althorn (a small tuba).

★　★　★

31. b. 1812. The United States was fighting the British again on our soil in The War of 1812. Begun mainly in response to British refusal to recognize American neutrality in the Napoleonic Wars, much of the fighting on land centered around the American-Canadian border. In August, 1814, the British burned Washington, D.C., including the White House and the Capitol.

★　★　★

32. d. 1888. When the nation was first founded, voting in some states was by voice, especially in the South. Names were called, and the voter answered with his choice of candidate. Sometimes voters' names were written in a book under the candidate's name. By the mid-1800's, most states were using written ballots, which were handed to an official or placed in a box. Written ballots gradually were replaced with printed ballots – printed by the political parties. This system presented problems, as voters could be intimidated by their own party. In 1888, Louisville, Kentucky was the first city to issue paper ballots printed by the local government rather than a political party.[8]

33. The expression "O.K." became popular with Martin van Buren's reelection campaign of 1840. For what did the letters "O.K." stand during the campaign?

a. Old Kerhonkson   b. Old Kanona
c. Old Kinderhook   d. Old Killawog

★ ★ ★

34. What was new in the campaign of 1896?

a. Loud speakers   b. Radio
c. Modern campaign buttons   d. Bumper stickers

★ ★ ★

35. In which Presidential election were voting machines first used?

a. 1860   b. 1872   c. 1892   d. 1904

★ ★ ★

36. To what party did Abraham Lincoln belong before becoming a Republican?

a. The Democratic Party   b. The Free Soil Party
c. The Liberty Party   d. The Whig Party

33. c. Old Kinderhook. The expression "O.K." had become popular at a time when the country was experiencing a craze for acronyms and humorous misspellings. It first appeared in print in the *Boston Post* in 1839 with reference to the phrase "oll correct," (sometimes spelled "oll korrect") meaning "all correct." Born in Kinderhook, New York, eighth President Martin van Buren was referred to as "Old Kinderhook" by his supporters. Democrats in New York City formed the O.K. Club to campaign for his reelection in 1840, further popularizing the term "O.K."[9] The expression "O.K." is still with us, but van Buren lost the election.   ★   ★   ★

34. c. Modern campaign buttons. There were political buttons at the time of George Washington; they had loops for attachment to clothing. Later campaign buttons, such as those with a likeness of Abraham Lincoln, were designed to be hung by a ribbon from the button hole of a coat lapel. The modern campaign buttons that we see today were first used in the campaign of 1896 between William McKinley and William Jennings Bryan.   ★   ★   ★

35. c. 1892. The first American voting machine featuring a counter to automatically count the votes was invented by Jacob H. Myers. It made its debut in Lockport, New York in 1892. While the voting machine was instrumental in eliminating voting fraud, its popularity was not instant.

Earlier American machines, and British-manufactured machines from as early as 1869, made use of balls which were released by each voter. However, the necessity to count the balls proved an obstacle to efficiency![10]
               ★   ★   ★

36. d. The Whig Party. Lincoln served as a Whig member of the Illinois House of Representatives from 1846-48. Former Whigs and others who were anti-slavery formed the Republican Party in 1854. In 1856, Lincoln helped found the Illinois Republican Party, and became the Republican Party's second Presidential candidate in 1860.

37. By the election of 1888, the Republican party was sometimes known as the G.O.P. The initials G.O.P. are widely known to stand for:

    a. Great Opportunity Party.   **b.** Great Old Party.
    c. Growing Old Party.   **d.** Grand Old Party.

★   ★   ★

38. Who was the only Speaker of the House of Representatives to be elected President?

    a. John Quincy Adams   **b.** James K. Polk
    c. William McKinley   **d.** Lyndon Johnson

★   ★   ★

39. Which candidate, known for his eloquence, was called the "Boy Orator of the Platte?"

    a. Harry Truman   **b.** Theodore Roosevelt
    c. William Jennings Bryan   **d.** Adlai Stevenson

★   ★   ★

40. Which candidate was criticized by opposition newspapers as being ugly?

    a. Zachary Taylor   **b.** Millard Fillmore
    c. James Buchanan   **d.** Abraham Lincoln

37. <u>d.</u> **Grand Old Party.** The initials "G.O.P." date back to the 1870's and 1880's. In 1875 the *Congressional Quarterly Record* made reference to "this gallant old party," and, according to *Harper's Weekly,* in 1876 the *Cincinnati Commercial* called it the "Grand Old Party." The letters "GOP" have stood for other things: in the early days of the automobile, it meant "get out and push!" "Go-Party" was used briefly in the 1964 campaign, "generation of peace" appeared during the Nixon administration, and once again "Grand Old Party" in the 1970's. The Democratic Party is actually the older of the two major parties, having been formed in the 1830's.[11]

The elephant first appeared as a Republican symbol in the campaign of 1860; the donkey was first used to represent the Democratic Party in the 1830's. Both were popularized as political symbols by famed cartoonist Thomas Nast in the 1870's and 1880's.

★ ★ ★

38. <u>b.</u> **James K. Polk.** The eleventh President, Polk served as Speaker of the House from 1835-1839, and was President from 1845-1849.

★ ★ ★

39. <u>c.</u> **William Jennings Bryan,** of Nebraska. However, according to his contemporary, Senator Joseph Foraker: in Nebraska the Platte River is "six inches deep and six miles wide at the mouth."[12]

★ ★ ★

40. <u>d.</u> **Abraham Lincoln.** But speaking on behalf of Lincoln at rallies, Dick Yates, Illinois candidate for governor, declared: "Well, if all the ugly men in the United States vote for him, he will surely be elected!"[13]

❧ *The Electoral College* ❧

41. **What is the Electoral College?**

    a. A body that counts the vote on election day
    b. A body chosen every four years to vote for President of the United States
    c. A body - whose members are appointed for life - that votes for President of the United States
    d. A college in Washington, D.C.

★   ★   ★

42. **Why was the Electoral College created by the founding fathers?**

    a. All of the founding fathers favored this system.
    b. We had had an electoral system for decades.
    c. It was a compromise solution for choosing the President.
    d. That system had worked in many countries.

★   ★   ★

43. **How is the number of electors/electoral votes determined for each state?**

    a. By agreement between the political parties
    b. By a joint session of Congress
    c. According to the number of Representatives from a state
    d. According to the total number of Representatives and Senators from a state

41. b. A body chosen every four years to vote for President of the United States. In this context, the term "college" refers to a decision-making group.

★   ★   ★

42. c. It was a compromise solution for choosing the President. At the Constitutional Convention, there were proposals to have the President chosen by a vote of Congress, by state legislatures and by popular vote. Each was voted down. It was felt that the President should be independent of and not be appointed by Congress; if state legislatures were to select the President, federal authority might be challenged. James Madison (who would become the fourth President) and others favored election of the president by popular vote. However, without widespread communications at the time, the founding fathers decided that voters would vote only for candidates known to them from their own state. This would favor the states with larger populations. The idea of state-by-state vote, as in the Electoral College, would give equal influence to the smaller states. At that time, Americans identified more closely with their state than with a national government. The original thirteen colonies were almost like thirteen different countries; the idea of one large country united by a national government and a constitution of laws was new.

The electoral system agreed upon was patterned in part after a system in use in Maryland (since 1776) for electing its state senators.

★   ★   ★

43. d. According to the total number of Representatives and Senators from a state. The total number of Representatives may change according to changes in population, which are calculated in the census every ten years.

44. How were the slaves originally counted in the population, determining a state's representation in the House of Representatives and in the Electoral College?

> **a.** Each slave was counted as 3/5's of a person.
> **b.** The slaves weren't counted in the population.
> **c.** Each slave was counted as one person.
> **d.** Every two slaves were counted as one person.

★   ★   ★

45. Who are members of the Electoral College?

> **a.** People nationally chosen to vote for President
> **b.** A slate of electors in each state that votes for their
>   own choice of President and Vice-President
> **c.** A slate of electors in each state that votes for President
>   and Vice-President according to the popular vote
>   of their state
> **d.** College graduates who vote for President in the
>   Electoral College

★   ★   ★

46. What are "pledged" electors?

> **a.** Electors who pledge loyalty to the United States
> **b.** Electors who are legally committed to vote for their
>   party's candidates for President and Vice-President
> **c.** Electors who pledge loyalty to their state
> **d.** Electors who have recited the Pledge of Allegiance

44. **a. Each slave was counted as 3/5's of a person.** Since electoral votes were distributed according to a state's population, the southern states favored counting each slave as one person in order to increase their state's representation in Congress and its number of electoral votes. This idea being opposed by the North at the Constitutional Convention, a debate ensued, and the delegates, settling on the Connecticut Compromise, agreed to count the slaves as 3/5's of their population.

This was officially overturned with the Fourteenth Amendment, enacted into law after the Civil War in 1868 – which counted "the whole number of persons in each State, excluding Indians not taxed."

★　★　★

45. **c. A slate of electors in each state that votes for President and Vice-President according to the popular vote of their state.** However, in our first elections, members of the Electoral College voted for whichever candidate they personally favored.

★　★　★

46. **b. Electors who are legally committed to vote for their party's candidates for President and Vice-President.** When we vote for President and Vice-President, we are actually voting for the slate of electors from our state. Each Presidential/Vice-Presidential ticket has a slate of electors that is expected to vote for them if their ticket wins the popular vote of a state. In about half of the states, electors are "pledged." The rest of the states have "unpledged" electors. Although not legally pledged to vote for their party's candidates, these electors are nonetheless expected to vote for the Presidential and Vice-Presidential candidates of their party. There have been just a handful of "faithless" electors out of approximately 20,000 electors since 1789. So far, this has not affected the outcome of an election, but there is no federal law against being a "faithless" elector.[14]

47. According to the Constitution, who is not eligible to be an elector?

>   **a.** Those who have previously served as electors
>   **b.** Members of a political party
>   **c.** Senators or Representatives or persons holding an office of trust or profit
>   **d.** People who are not members of a political party

★   ★   ★

48. Where does the Electoral College meet?

>   **a.** In their respective states   **b.** Washington, D.C.
>   **c.** New York   **d.** Philadelphia

★   ★   ★

49. In a Presidential election year, the Electoral College meets on:

>   **a.** election day
>   **b.** the first Monday after the second Wednesday in December
>   **c.** December 1st
>   **d.** December 12th

47. c. **Senators or Representatives or persons holding an office of trust or profit.** According to Article II, Section I of the Constitution, "…no Senator or Representative, or Person holding an Office of Trust or Profit under the United States, shall be appointed an Elector." This is generally taken today to mean that no one holding public office is eligible to be an elector. The Fourteenth Amendment adds that "No person shall be … (an) "elector of President and Vice-President" who has "engaged in insurrection or rebellion" against the United States.

★   ★   ★

48. a. **In their respective states.** In most states they meet – by state law – in their state capitals. The electors never actually come together from across the nation to vote as a group.

★   ★   ★

49. b. **the first Monday after the second Wednesday in December.** Originally set by Congress for the first Wednesday in December, the date was moved in 1877 to the second Monday in January, which allowed for more time to settle election disputes. In 1934, Congress changed the date to the first Monday after the second Wednesday in December. The electors usually meet at noon.

50. When did the term "Electoral College" first appear?

    a. In 1787, in the Constitution   **b.** In 1789
    c. In the early 1800's   **d.** In the early 1900's

★   ★   ★

51. Following a Presidential election, the results of the Electoral College vote are officially announced on:

    a. January 1st   **b.** January 6th
    c. January 10th   **d.** January 20th

★   ★   ★

52. According to the Constitution, who decides how electors are to be chosen?

    a. State legislatures   **b.** Political parties
    c. The House of Representatives   **d.** The Senate

★   ★   ★

53. Today, forty-eight of the fifty states have a "winner-take-all" system of awarding electoral votes. Which two states divide their electoral votes?

    a. Colorado and Washington   **b.** Vermont and Maine
    c. Minnesota and Oregon   **d.** Maine and Nebraska

50. **c. In the early 1800's.** The term "Electoral College" does not appear in the Constitution. It came into unofficial use during the early 1800's, and was used officially starting in 1845.

★   ★   ★

51. **b. January 6th (or the 7th if the 6th falls on a Sunday).** The votes are counted in Washington, D.C. by members of Congress appointed to count the votes in a joint session of Congress. The results are then read by the president of the Senate – who is also the Vice-President of the United States.

★   ★   ★

52. **a. State legislatures.** Article II, Section I states: "Each state shall appoint, in such Manner as the Legislature thereof may direct, a Number of Electors…"

In our early elections, they were chosen in each state by popular vote at large, by popular vote by district, or by the state legislature. While at first electors were chosen in many states by the state legislature, by 1828 most states had adopted popular election of presidential electors. South Carolina was the last state to change to popular election of its electors, in the 1860's.

★   ★   ★

53. **d. Maine and Nebraska.** On election day, forty-eight of the fifty states vote for a candidate's slate of electors by direct statewide election. The winner takes all. In 1969, Maine – and in 1991, Nebraska – decided to choose two electors by statewide popular vote, and the rest by popular vote in each Congressional district.

54. In our first Presidential elections, electors had two votes each for President. The runner-up in electoral votes:

      a. became Speaker of the House.
      b. became Secretary of State.
      c. became Vice-President.
      d. did not win any office or appointment.

★ ★ ★

55. How many states cast electoral votes in the first Presidential election?

      a. 10   **b.** 11   **c.** 12   **d.** 13

★ ★ ★

56. According to the Constitution, who decides the winner of the Vice-Presidency in the event that no candidate wins a majority in the Electoral College?

      a. The Electoral College   **b.** The House of Representatives
      c. The Senate   **d.** The Supreme Court

★ ★ ★

57. According to the Constitution, who decides the winner of the Presidency in the event that no candidate wins a majority in the Electoral College?

      a. The Electoral College   **b.** The House of Representatives
      c. The Senate   **d.** The Supreme Court

54. **c. became Vice-President.** However, the founding fathers didn't foresee the possible problems with this voting arrangement, as a President and Vice-President from two different parties could be elected. This happened in 1796. The Twelfth Amendment to the Constitution, which took effect on September 25, 1804, directed the electors to vote separately for President and Vice-President. The Twelfth Amendment also designated March 4th as the date a Presidential term expired. This provision was superceded by the Twentieth Amendment, ratified January 23, 1933, which set the date of expiration of the President's term as January 20th.

★   ★   ★

55. **a. 10.** Of the original thirteen states, Connecticut, Georgia, Delaware, Maryland, Massachusetts, New Hampshire, New Jersey, Pennsylvania, South Carolina and Virginia voted. North Carolina and Rhode Island had not yet ratified the Constitution, and the legislature in New York State couldn't decide how to choose its electors in time for the election.

★   ★   ★

56. **c. The Senate.** Each Senator has one vote. In 1836, Democrat Martin van Buren won the Presidency, but his Vice-Presidential candidate Richard M. Johnson failed to receive a majority in the Electoral College. He was unpopular in the South for marrying a slave and raising their children as free people; Virginia's electors would not vote for him, denying him an electoral majority. The Senate met – the only time in history – to decide the Vice-Presidential race. They voted and decided in Johnson's favor, 33-16.[15]

★   ★   ★

57. **b. The House of Representatives.** Originally, if no candidate won a majority of electoral votes, the House would choose from between the top five candidates, with one vote per state. The Twelfth Amendment, ratified on June 15, 1804, changed that provision from the top five candidates to the top three. A quorum of two-thirds of the states is necessary to vote, and a candidate must receive a majority in order to win. The Twelfth Amendment also provided for separate balloting for President and Vice-President.

58. Presidents John Quincy Adams, Rutherford B. Hayes and Benjamin Harrison lost the popular vote but won the electoral vote. So far there has been one other person who lost the popular vote and won the election. Who was that candidate?

       a. Andrew Jackson   **b.** Abraham Lincoln
       c. Harry Truman   **d.** George W. Bush

★ ★ ★

59. When the Senate met to officially count the 2004 Electoral College results, a protest was registered to draw attention to voting irregularities in what state?

       a. Ohio   **b.** Florida
       c. Pennsylvania   **d.** Minnesota

★ ★ ★

60. Which state has the most electoral votes?

       a. Texas   **b.** California
       c. New York   **d.** Florida

★ ★ ★

61. What is the total number of electoral votes at this time?

       a. 536   **b.** 538   **c.** 540   **d.** 542

58. d. George W. Bush. In 2000, Bush lost the popular vote by approximately 540,000 votes, but secured an electoral vote majority, 271 to 266.

★ ★ ★

59. a. Ohio. In an effort to draw attention to voting irregularities in Ohio, two Democrats – the required one Representative and one Senator - forced a challenge to the electoral vote count, which by law requires the House and Senate to meet separately to debate the issue for up to two hours. The hope was to highlight problems - such as excessively long lines at the polls and missing voting machines - that occurred primarily in minority neighborhoods during the 2004 election. This was only the second time since 1877 (when the Hayes/Tilden vote of 1876 was debated) that the counting of the electoral vote was interrupted. In 1969 the House and Senate met separately to discuss a "faithless" elector who had voted for George Wallace instead of Richard Nixon. Congress allowed the vote to be counted.

60. b. California. It has 55 electoral votes. The next three states with the most votes are: Texas: 34, New York: 31 and Florida: 27.

★ ★ ★

61. b. 538: 100 Senators, (two from each state) plus 435 Representatives from the states, plus three Representatives from the District of Columbia. The Twenty-third Amendment to the Constitution gave voters in the District of Columbia the right to appoint electors equal to the number of Representatives (1) and Senators (2) it would have if it were a state. The District of Columbia has one Representative in the House of Representatives who votes in committees, but does not have the right to vote for or against bills in Congress.

62. **Who received the most popular votes?**

      a. Lyndon Johnson   **b.** Richard Nixon
      c. Ronald Reagan   **d.** George W. Bush

★   ★   ★

63. **Who received the most electoral votes?**

      a. Lyndon Johnson   **b.** Richard Nixon
      c. Ronald Reagan   **d.** George W. Bush

★   ★   ★

64. **Who received the biggest electoral vote majority?**

      a. Franklin D. Roosevelt   **b.** Richard Nixon
      c. Lyndon Johnson   **d.** Ronald Reagan

★   ★   ★

65. **Who was the only President to be elected unanimously by the Electoral College?**

      a. George Washington   **b.** Thomas Jefferson
      c. Abraham Lincoln   **d.** Franklin D. Roosevelt

62. d. George W. Bush. In 2004, Republican incumbent George W. Bush received over 62 million votes. John Kerry, the Democratic candidate, also received more popular votes – over 59 million - than any previous Presidential candidate.

★ ★ ★

63. c. Ronald Reagan. In 1984 he received 525 votes.

★ ★ ★

64. a. Franklin D. Roosevelt In 1936, Roosevelt received 523 electoral votes to 8 for Republican Alf Landon, a 515 vote majority.

★ ★ ★

65. a. George Washington. Washington received 69 votes in 1789 and 132 votes in 1792. Electors were able to vote for two Presidential candidates at the time; each elector cast one of his votes for him in both 1789 and 1792. Washington was the only President to receive a vote from every elector.

There was really no contest for President in 1789. Everyone expected George Washington to be elected. With electors in several states giving their second vote to favorite sons from their own state, the contest was for Vice-President. (Just to be sure that John Adams didn't tie Washington in the electoral vote, Alexander Hamilton told electors from several states to withhold their second vote from Adams). As a result, there was a long list of people – twelve - who received electoral votes in 1789. John Adams, with 34 votes, came in second behind Washington, and became Vice-President.

There was a possible total of 91 electoral votes in 1789. However, Rhode Island (three votes) and North Carolina (seven votes) had not yet ratified the Constitution, and New York could not agree on how to select its eight electors in time for the election. In addition, two electors from Maryland and two from Virginia were not present at the voting on February 4th. 69 electors voted for President in 1789.[16]

The Elections, the Campaigns,

ℰ   and the Issues   ℅

THE ELECTIONS, THE CAMPAIGNS,
★ ★ ★ _AND THE ISSUES_ ★ ★ ★

_1789_

66. What kind of campaign did George Washington conduct?

a. He traveled around the country shaking hands with many Americans.
b. He gave campaign speeches in the major cities.
c. He did no campaigning.
d. He hired political consultants.

★ ★ ★

67. Which political party nominated George Washington for President?

a. Democratic   **b.** Republican
c. Federalist   **d.** None

★ ★ ★

68. Where was George Washington inaugurated in 1789?

a. New York   **b.** Philadelphia
c. Mount Vernon   **d.** Washington, D.C.

66. c. He did no campaigning. Admired for his moral character and respected by people of different political beliefs, Washington was the obvious choice to be the young country's first President. Widely known as a hero of the Revolution, he didn't need to campaign. Indeed, it would have been considered undignified to do so in those days. Washington received word on April 14, 1789 that the electoral votes had been counted by the Senate and that he had been elected, receiving a vote from all 69 electors who voted. He was sworn in on April 30th. Congress was scheduled to begin its first session on March 4th, but had to wait until a quorum was present on April 6th to convene.[17]

★   ★   ★

67. d. None. There were no organized political parties then - no conventions, no nominating speeches, no campaigns – just rallies of support for George Washington on the 4th of July in 1788.[18] His belief in an active central government for the young country was shared by those in the emerging Federalist Party – which included John Adams and Alexander Hamilton. After the Constitutional Convention of 1787, those who advocated that the states should ratify the Constitution were known as Federalists, while those who believed the Constitution gave too much authority to the federal government were against ratification, and were known as Anti-Federalists.

★   ★   ★

68. a. New York. In 1789, Washington was inaugurated at Federal Hall in New York, the country's first capital. The young government moved to Philadelphia in 1790, and finally to the newly designed capital city of Washington, D. C. in 1800.

George Washington wasn't entirely enthusiastic about becoming President. He wanted to be home at Mount Vernon, he felt his health was not as good as it used to be, and he dreaded undertaking an immense new responsibility for which he did not think himself properly equipped. "My movements to the chair of government will be accompanied by feelings not unlike those of a culprit who is going to the place of his execution."[19]

1792

69. George Washington had planned to serve one term as President and return to Mount Vernon after four years. However, rival political factions had developed during his Presidency, and many people felt he was needed to hold the young country together. Washington decided to stand for election to a second term. Who was the leader of the opposition?

> **a.** Thomas Jefferson   **b.** John Adams
> **c.** Aaron Burr   **d.** James Madison

★ ★ ★

70. What did everyone view as a signal that Washington would agree to serve a second term?

> **a.** He announced that he would consider it.
> **b.** He published a letter in a newspaper about it.
> **c.** He asked his Cabinet for their blessing.
> **d.** He was silent on the issue.

★ ★ ★

71. How did Washington feel about the adversarial nature of the developing political factions?

> **a.** He encouraged it.   **b.** He didn't comment on it.
> **c.** He was opposed to it.   **d.** He was unaware of it.

1792

69. **a. Thomas Jefferson.** Jefferson strongly favored states' rights, while George Washington believed the country needed a strong central government. The two main political factions were not political parties as we know them today; nevertheless, there was much heated debate between them, which made this period in our history very partisan. Leading the forces in agreement with Washington was his Secretary of State, Alexander Hamilton. They favored a strong central government, a Treasury that had an important role in the country's economic life, and were pro-British in their foreign policy. Jefferson's followers advocated limited central government, limited government influence in economic matters, and were pro-French. Despite their differences, members of both political factions felt that Washington should serve a second term in order to hold the young republic together.

Washington was sworn in on March 4, 1793. March 4th would remain the inauguration date until 1937, when it was changed to January 20th.

★ ★ ★

70. **d. He was silent on the issue.** Everyone assumed this meant Washington would stand for reelection. He did, and was reelected unanimously, receiving votes from all 132 electors. John Adams – with 77 electoral votes – once again became Vice-President.

★ ★ ★

71. c. He was opposed to it. However, even George Washington was unable to prevent the emergence of opposing factions. He served a second term, but that only delayed the start of the two party system – with many an adversarial campaign to follow!

1796

72. The leading candidates in 1796 were Federalist John Adams and Republican Thomas Jefferson. Partisanship was alive and well, with both sides hurling attacks. Jeffersonians claimed Adams lacked faith in the people and was " 'an avowed friend of monarchy' who plotted to make his sons 'Seigneurs or Lords of this country.' "[20] Adams' followers called Jefferson an "atheist, anarchist, demagogue, coward, mountebank" (quack medicine salesman!), "trickster and Franco-maniac," claiming his followers were "cut-throats who walk in rags and sleep amongst filth and vermin!"[21]

Adams won. Who became his Vice-President?

    a. James Madison   **b.** Aaron Burr
    c. Alexander Hamilton   **d.** Thomas Jefferson

★   ★   ★

73. A major issue in the election of 1796 concerned a controversial treaty negotiated with the British government in 1794. What was this treaty called?

    a. The Jefferson Treaty   **b.** The Adams Treaty
    c. The Jay Treaty   **d.** The British Treaty

★   ★   ★

74. Another campaign issue of 1796 involved a rebellion of farmers in western Pennsylvania in 1794. By what name is this rebellion known?

    a. The Tax Rebellion   **b.** The Farmer's Rebellion
    c. The Pennsylvania Rebellion   **d.** The Whiskey Rebellion

1796

72. **d. Thomas Jefferson.** Yes, Jefferson the "atheist, anarchist, trickster," etc. and leader of the newly formed Republican Party, (not the Republican Party of today) became Vice-President. He received 68 electoral votes to 71 for John Adams. According to the Constitution at the time, Jefferson, in second place, became Vice-President. A total of thirteen people received electoral votes in 1796, including George Washington, who received 2 votes.

★   ★   ★

73. **c. The Jay Treaty.** In spite of the Treaty of Paris of 1783, which ended the Revolutionary War, the British were still causing problems. There were unpaid war reparations, they were occupying U.S. western military posts in the Northwest Territory, trading fur in the Great Lakes region and impressing American sailors in the Caribbean into British service. President Washington sent John Jay - whom he had appointed as the first Chief Justice of the Supreme Court - to London to negotiate with the British. He returned with a treaty, but it was unpopular with many Americans, and was sharply criticized by Jeffersonians, as the British did not agree to end impressments of American sailors who were former British subjects, or to end search and seizure of American ships delivering goods to enemies of Britain. They only agreed to vacate their forts in the Northwest, which they had already agreed to in 1783. The Jay Treaty, however, was ratified by the U.S. Senate in 1795.

★   ★   ★

74. **d. The Whiskey Rebellion.** In 1794, farmers in western Pennsylvania were unhappy with a federal tax (to help repay Revolutionary War debts) on whiskey. They refused to pay the tax. Tax collectors met with violent resistance, which led the federal government to send 15,000 army troops to the area. George Washington himself came to view the troops and settle the dispute – peacefully – but the rebellion remained an issue with regard to federal authority vs. states' rights. Republicans objected to this "show of force" meant to enforce national authority. 150 suspects were arrested, and two of them received death sentences, both of which were repealed by Washington.

1800

75. For this election, the Republicans organized the first:

    a. state parties.　　　　　**b.** debates.
    c. state conventions.　　　 **d.** state fairs.

★　　★　　★

76. Vice-President Jefferson challenged President Adams in 1800. Jefferson was intensely opposed to the Alien and Sedition Acts, which were passed into law and signed by John Adams. What were these acts?

    a. Laws raising taxes
    b. More lenient immigration laws
    c. More lenient laws regarding free speech
    d. Acts limiting immigration and freedom of the press

★　　★　　★

77. In 1799, Federalists asked George Washington to:

    a. campaign for Federalist President John Adams.
    b. make a farewell tour of the United States.
    c. run for President again.
    d. speak on behalf of all Federalist candidates.

75. a. state parties. Thomas Jefferson and the Republican Party led the opposition to Alexander Hamilton and the Federalists' support of a strong central government. Jefferson and his followers, who favored small business and an agrarian society where the hands of power rested with the common people, distrusted power in a central government. The Republicans evolved from the Anti-Federalists, who feared the Constitution entrusted too much power to the federal government.

★ ★ ★

76. d. Acts limiting immigration and freedom of the press. George Washington's pro-British policies led to the threat of a possible war with France. In response to this threat, and in an effort to suppress the Republican opposition, John Adams signed into law four bills from Congress in 1798. The first one, the Naturalization Act, made it more difficult for immigrants (mostly Jeffersonians) to become citizens by changing the residence requirement for citizenship from five to fourteen years; the Alien Act enabled the President to deport any alien who was considered dangerous; the Alien Enemies Act authorized the arrest, imprisonment and deportation of enemy aliens during wartime, and the Sedition Act threatened to fine or imprison anyone who "shall write, print, utter or publish any false, scandalous and malicious writing or writings against the government of the United States." Twenty-five men, most of them editors of the opposition press, were imprisoned. When he became President, Thomas Jefferson pardoned them all. Their fines – with interest – were repaid by Congress. Three of the Alien and Sedition Acts lapsed in 1800, and the fourth was repealed in 1802.

★ ★ ★

77. c. run for President again. He declined, stating that party politics now ruled the day, and that character and individuality were no longer important. Washington claimed that "the parties could now 'set up a broomstick' and get it elected…"[22]

1800

78. Thomas Jefferson received 73 electoral votes. Who received exactly the same number of votes, forcing the decision into the House of Representatives?

        a. John Adams   **b.** Aaron Burr
        c. Charles C. Pinckney   **d.** John Jay

★   ★   ★

79. Who intervened behind-the-scenes in the vote of the House of Representatives?

        a. John Adams   **b.** Aaron Burr
        c. Alexander Hamilton   **d.** James Madison

★   ★   ★

80. With the election of 1800, the United States prepared for its first:

        a. Vice-President that became President.
        b. inaugural parade.
        c. President from Virginia.
        d. transfer of power from one party to another.

1800

78. **b. Aaron Burr.** Former U.S. Senator Aaron Burr of New York, who was considered the Republican Vice-Presidential candidate, (and was Jefferson's choice because he could carry New York for the Republicans) tied Jefferson. Each received 73 electoral votes. Believing he might have a chance to win the Presidency, Burr refused to defer to Jefferson. According to the Constitution, in the event that no one wins a majority, the House of Representatives decides the winner, with one vote per state. It took 36 ballots before the election was decided by the House – in favor of Jefferson – on February 17th, 1801. Burr became Vice-President. Incumbent John Adams received 65 votes. This experience led to the passage of the Twelfth Amendment, which provides for separate ballots for President and Vice-President in the Electoral College. With the development of political parties, candidates ran as a team after 1800.

★ ★ ★

79. **c. Alexander Hamilton.** A leading Federalist, Hamilton could see that Federalist John Adams was not going to be reelected. The choice was between Jefferson and Burr. Feeling that Thomas Jefferson was the lesser of two evils, Hamilton used his influence in the House to swing the election to Jefferson.

★ ★ ★

80. **d. transfer of power from one party to another.** The election featured bitter attacks in the press from both sides, and intense partisanship. The Federalists had held the White House for the first three terms of the young country's Presidency. Now their opponent, Thomas Jefferson, was to become President. Some Federalists actually threatened to block Jefferson's inauguration. When the Virginia militia threatened to march on Washington, the Federalists backed down, and, on March 4, 1801, the United States completed its first peaceful transfer of power from one party to another. [23]

1804

81. Federalist Charles C. Pinckney of South Carolina challenged President Jefferson, who was enjoying immense popularity due to peace and prosperity, lower taxes, a reduction in the national debt, a cut in defense spending and what other major accomplishment?

    a. The founding of the University of Virginia
    b. The Louisiana Purchase
    c. Inventing the polygraph copying machine
    d. Designing his home, Monticello

★   ★   ★

82. Jefferson and the Republicans dropped Vice-President Aaron Burr from the ticket in 1804. Burr had refused to defer to Jefferson in the electoral tie in 1800, and in addition had gained notoriety for:

    a. killing Alexander Hamilton in a duel.
    b. gambling.
    c. criticizing Jefferson.
    d. switching parties.

★   ★   ★

83. Which of the following did Thomas Jefferson do after being elected (and serving as) President?

    a. He started building his home "Monticello."
    b. He drafted the Virginia Statute for Religious Freedom.
    c. He served as Minister (Ambassador) to France.
    d. He founded the University of Virginia.

1804

81. b. The Louisiana Purchase. On April 3, 1803, Jefferson purchased the Louisiana Territory from Napoleon, who was close to war with Britain and in need of money. The territory became all or part of fifteen states. For $11,250,000 plus responsibility for $3,750,000 in claims by American citizens against France, Jefferson doubled the size of the country. The United States gained 800,000 square miles, stretching from New Orleans to the Rocky Mountains.[24] Federalists questioned Jefferson's constitutional authority to purchase the Louisiana Territory; some viewed it as a threat to the influence of New England, and took the issue to the Supreme Court. The court ruled that the Louisiana Purchase was Constitutional in *American Insurance Company vs. Canter* in 1828.

★   ★   ★

82. a. killing Alexander Hamilton in a duel. Burr had been repeatedly criticized - in public and in private - by Hamilton, and finally challenged him to a duel. On July 11, 1804, in Weehawken, New Jersey, Aaron Burr fatally shot Alexander Hamilton. For the election of 1804 Burr was replaced as the Republican Vice-Presidential candidate by George Clinton, the first Governor of New York. Jefferson and Clinton garnered votes from traditionally Federalist New England, and won with 162 electoral votes to 14 for their Federalist opponents, Charles C. Pinckney and Rufus King.

★   ★   ★

83. d. He founded the University of Virginia. The university opened in 1825. Jefferson began the construction of Monticello (1770), drafted the Virginia Statute of Religious Freedom (written in 1779, approved while he was in France in 1786) and served as Minister to France (1785-89) before serving as President from 1801-1809.

1808

84. Federalist Charles C. Pinckney made another run for the Presidency, this time opposed by Republican Secretary of State James Madison of Virginia. Madison is known as:

    a. The Father of his country.
    b. The Father of Liberty.
    c. The Father of the Constitution.
    d. The Father of the Democratic Party.

★   ★   ★

85. As a member of the Jefferson administration, Madison faced attacks during the election regarding legislation passed in response to harassment of American ships. It was much talked about during the campaign. What was this legislation called?

    a. The Madison Act   **b.** The Neutrality Act
    c. The Embargo of 1807   **d.** The Blockade of 1807

★   ★   ★

86. When James Madison ran for President, he was well-known for playing a major role at the Constitutional Convention of 1787. In addition, he was known for helping to win ratification of the Constitution by writing newspaper articles known as:

    a. The papers of 1787.   **b.** The Federalist Papers.
    c. The Constitution Papers.   **d.** The Madison Papers.

1808

84. **c. Father of the Constitution.** During the Constitutional Convention of 1787 in Philadelphia, Madison seated himself in the middle of the proceedings in order to be able to hear everyone. His detailed notes are the definitive source of information on the deliberations there. As a delegate, Madison spoke in favor of a strong central government for the United States. Years later, in 1834, Madison wrote to a friend: "You give me a credit to which I have no claim, in calling me '*the* writer of the Constitution of the United States.' This was not, like the fabled Goddess, the offspring of a single brain. It ought to be regarded as the work of many heads & many hands."[25] Madison won, 122 to 47 electoral votes. Independent George Clinton received 6 votes. ★ ★ ★

85. **c. The Embargo of 1807.** During the Napoleonic Wars, British and French ships were seizing and harassing American ships headed for each other's ports. Under the Embargo of 1807, American ports were closed to foreign shipping, but the Embargo backfired, as many Americans lost their jobs. Some manufacturers prospered due to decreased foreign trade, but farm surpluses weren't used, and the original intent – to win U.S. neutral rights at sea – was not accomplished. The Embargo was then changed to include only Britain and France. It was repealed by Congress before Thomas Jefferson left office.[26]
★ ★ ★

86. b. The Federalist Papers. Using the pen name of "Publius" (a famous defender of the Roman Republic) Federalists James Madison, Alexander Hamilton and John Jay sent essays to New York newspapers, urging citizens there to vote for ratification of the new constitution. "Anti-federalist" papers voiced concerns about   the new constitution: dangers from tyranny not adequately addressed, objections to a standing army, federal power vs. state authority, dangers of foreign and civil wars, taxation, and the power of the judiciary were just a few of the issues raised. The Federalist Papers appeared from October, 1787 to May, 1788.

1812

87. Madison easily won re-nomination for a second term. Former New York City mayor DeWitt Clinton – a Federalist backed Republican – opposed him. What issue dominated the campaign?

    a. The War of 1812   **b.** The Tariff
    c. Immigration   **d.** The Louisiana Purchase

★   ★   ★

88. Those opposed to Madison's reelection pointed out that since three of the first four Presidents were Virginians, the state of Virginia was disproportionately represented in the White House. They referred to this as:

    a. The Virginia Monopoly.   **b.** The Virginia Plan.
    c. The Virginia Dynasty.   **d.** The Virginia Presidents.

★   ★   ★

89. Madison's Vice-Presidential candidate was Massachusetts Governor Elbridge Gerry. As governor, Gerry drew up a redistricting plan for Massachusetts which included some odd-shaped districts designed to favor election of Republicans to state offices. What term was invented by a newspaper editor of the time that signifies the use of redistricting for political advantage?

    a. Political redistricting   **b.** Gerrymandering
    c. Partisan redistricting   **d.** Gerrydistricting

1812

87. **a. The War of 1812.** Fought in response to impressment of American sailors and interference in American trade by the British, The War of 1812 aimed to defend our neutral rights at sea, to force the British out of Canada, to force Spain out of Florida and to increase the size of the country. There was much disagreement regarding the idea of going to war; many were opposed to it. In 1815, at the end of the war, General Andrew Jackson gained fame for defeating the British at New Orleans, not knowing that a peace treaty – the Treaty of Ghent – had already been signed.

★ ★ ★

88. **c. The Virginia Dynasty.** Although they were not all political allies, the first three Virginia Presidents – Washington, Jefferson and Madison - were referred to as the "Virginia Dynasty."

★ ★ ★

89. **b. Gerrymandering.** As governor, Elbridge Gerry used his influence to design new districts in Massachusetts to favor the election of Republicans. The shape of one district was very odd. Comparing its shape to that of a salamander, the editor of the *Boston Centinel* coined the term "gerrymander."[27] The terms "gerrymander" and "gerrymandering" are still used to describe redistricting for political advantage.

Madison and Gerry won the election, 128 to 89 electoral votes.

1816

90. Secretary of State James Monroe of Virginia was the Republican candidate for President. The Federalists were in decline. Their opposition to what major issue contributed to their demise?

        a. The National Bank   **b.** The Louisiana Purchase
        c. The Embargo   **d.** The War of 1812

★ ★ ★

91. Although not officially nominated, Senator Rufus King of New York was supported by the Federalists. Monroe was presented by his supporters as having fought alongside George Washington, and as:

    a. the last "framer of the Constitution" still active.
    b. "a common man."
    c. "a leader for the future."
    d. "a great American."

★ ★ ★

92. In 1816 Republicans marched in parades and sang a new song entitled:

        a. Yankee Doodle.   **b.** America the Beautiful.
        c. Hail Columbia.   **d.** The Star Spangled Banner.

1816

90. d. The War of 1812. Many Federalist policies had been taken over by others. In addition, the secret meeting of New England Federalists to protest the war and to discuss the right of states to nullify federal laws - in particular, a law to draft citizens into a national army - ended their influence in national affairs.

★ ★ ★

91. a. the last "framer of the Constitution" still active. Although Monroe had opposed its ratification, he was portrayed as a "framer" of the Constitution. He won, 183 to 34 electoral votes.

★ ★ ★

92. d. The Star Spangled Banner. After setting fire to Washington, D.C. during the War of 1812, the British proceeded to Baltimore, where they aimed their cannons at Fort McHenry. Attorneys Francis Scott Key and John Skinner had boarded the British ship "HMS Tonnant" to negotiate the release of an elderly American who had been captured, Dr. William Beanes. Key's letters from wounded British soldiers telling of the good care they received from the Americans convinced the British to release Beanes. Key, Skinner and Beanes were told to wait in a small boat while, on September 13, 1814, the British commenced firing on Fort McHenry. As the battle raged into the night, they watched British rockets blazing through the sky, and bombs exploding in mid-air. With the light from "the rockets' red glare" and "the bombs bursting in air," the Americans were able to distinguish the giant American flag waving in the night sky over the fort. Finally, all was quiet, and, "by the dawn's early light" they could see "that our flag was still there." The British had decided that Fort McHenry wasn't worth the fight, and had given up. Being an amateur poet, Key penned four verses regaling the events of the night, and suggested that his poem be set to the tune of "To Anacraeon in Heaven" by British composer John Stafford Smith. The new song was very popular, but it was many years before it became our national anthem - in 1931.[28] The "Star Spangled Banner" that flew over Fort McHenry is 30' x 42'. It is kept at the Smithsonian's Museum of American History.

1820

<u>93.</u> Enjoying the widest popularity since George Washington, President Monroe ran for reelection. With former Federalists joining the Republicans, the two-party system gave way to a one-party system. The old two-party animosity had disappeared from the American political scene. This period in our history is referred to as:

    a. The Era of Peace.   **b.** The Era of Good Feelings.
    c. The Era of Reconciliation.   **d.** The Era of Goodwill.

★ ★ ★

<u>94.</u> Who ran against Monroe in 1820?

    a. John Quincy Adams   **b.** Andrew Jackson
    c. Henry Clay   **d.** No one

★ ★ ★

<u>95.</u> There was opposition to Monroe's re-nomination within his own party. The United States had experienced its first recession (1819-1821) due to poor banking practices, land speculation out west and competition from the resumption of European imports after the War of 1812. In addition, a law admitting Maine as a free state and Missouri as a slave state had become extremely controversial. What was the name of this law?

    a. The Compromise   **b.** The Monroe Compromise
    c. The Missouri Compromise   **d.** The Maine Compromise

1820

93. **b. The Era of Good Feelings.**

★ ★ ★

94. **d. No one.** Monroe received 231 electoral votes out of 232 votes cast. One elector, Governor William Plumer of New Hampshire, voted for Secretary of State John Quincy Adams, leaving George Washington the only president to be elected unanimously by the Electoral College. Plumer explained in his papers that he voted for Adams for President because "he is in every respect qualified for that high trust. Mr. Monroe during the last four years has, in my opinion, conducted, as president, very improperly." Plumer complained that the country needed "the internal taxes and duties" that Monroe had recommended for repeal, and that he had unnecessarily spent too much money "by granting pensions, ...increasing the pay of congress, & the salaries of civil officers..." He wrote that instead of paying the public debt, the government was compelled to borrow three million dollars, to be repaid in twelve years. Therefore, he could not vote for Monroe.[29]

Plumer also refused to support Vice-President Daniel Tompkins for reelection, whom he said, in his duties as President of the Senate, "receives an annual salary of five thousand dollars; during the last three years he was absent from the senate during their session nearly three fourths of the time ... He has not that weight of character which his office requires - the fact is he is grossly intemperate. I cannot vote for him to be again Vice-president – my vote will be given to Richard Rush, whom I have every reason to believe is well qualified for that office."[30]

★ ★ ★

95. **c. The Missouri Compromise.** Monroe was able to convince his fellow Republicans in Virginia that the Missouri Compromise was necessary for the survival of the United States, and, in so doing, gained their support.

1824

96. There were no political parties in 1824. Four regional candidates ran for President: John Quincy Adams of Massachusetts, William H. Crawford of Georgia, and two favorite sons: Senator Andrew Jackson of Tennessee and Henry Clay of Kentucky. What was unusual about the electoral vote count of 1824?

  a. Two candidates were tied.
  b. Three candidates were tied.
  c. Many electors didn't vote.
  d. The eventual winner, John Quincy Adams, had fifteen
    fewer electoral votes than Andrew Jackson.

★   ★   ★

97. When Henry Clay ran for President in 1824, he was:

  a. Speaker of the House.   **b.** a U.S. Senator.
  c. a lawyer in private practice.   **d.** Ambassador to Britain.

★   ★   ★

98. The Jackson campaign published the first:

  a. political magazine.   **b.** political jokes.
  c. campaign songbook.   **d.** campaign biography.

1824

96. d. **The eventual winner, John Quincy Adams, had fifteen fewer electoral votes than Andrew Jackson.** The vote was Jackson: 99, Adams: 84, Crawford: 41, Clay: 37. No one had an electoral vote majority. According to the Constitution, the names of the top three candidates went to the House of Representatives, where each state had one vote. However, Clay gave his support to Adams, who then gained the votes of six more states and was declared the winner. Adams proceeded to appoint Clay Secretary of State, which led Jackson's supporters to claim, "Corrupt bargain!" The previous three Presidents, Jefferson, Madison and Monroe (and John Quincy Adams) had been Secretary of State prior to being elected President; that office was regarded as a stepping stone to the Presidency. As it turned out, Henry Clay never became President.

Former Representative John C. Calhoun of South Carolina (Secretary of War in the Monroe administration) won the Vice-Presidency, receiving 182 electoral votes.

★   ★   ★

97. a. **Speaker of the House.** Clay served as Speaker three times, from 1811-14, 1815-20 and 1823-25. He also served in the Senate twice, from 1831-42 and 1849-52.

★   ★   ★

98. d. **Campaign biography.** Jackson's supporters referred to him as "a man of the people."

As a general, he was nicknamed "Hickory" by his men for being tough, and eventually became known as "Old Hickory."

Personal attacks abounded in this campaign without fundamental issues and party loyalties: "Adams' habits of dress and conduct were criticized; Calhoun was pictured as a young man consumed with ambition; Clay was by some accounts a drunkard and gambler; Crawford's honesty was questioned; and Jackson was to his opponents a mere military chieftain."[31]

1828

99. Shortly after the inauguration of John Quincy Adams in 1825, followers of Andrew Jackson founded a party – with organizers in every state. Originally referred to as "Friends of Jackson," the party eventually became known as:

      a. The Whig Party.   **b.** The Jacksonian Party.
      c. The Democratic Party.   **d.** The Libertarian Party.

★   ★   ★

100. Four years after their controversial contest of 1824, Andrew Jackson challenged incumbent John Quincy Adams. The voter turnout in 1828 – over 1.1 million – was more than three times the turnout of 1824. This was due in part to population growth and to:

      a. fewer voter eligibility requirements.
      b. good weather on election day.
      c. better communication among voters.
      d. more announcements in the newspapers.

★   ★   ★

101. With Andrew Jackson's election in 1828, he became the first President that was:

      a. a "westerner.
      b. born an American subject.
      c. born in a big city.
      d. inaugurated at the White House.

1828

99. **c. The Democratic Party.** First referred to as the Democratic-Republican Party, the party grew out of Jefferson's Republicans, and officially became known as the Democratic Party at their convention of 1840. Nominated by the Tennessee legislature in 1825 for the 1828 election, Jackson ran with incumbent John C. Calhoun (who was already serving as John Quincy Adams' Vice-President) as his running mate. Adams ran as the candidate of the National Republicans, a party that included his conservative supporters and former Federalists, with Richard Rush of Pennsylvania as his new running mate. They favored federal involvement in economic development. Jackson carried the West and the South, defeating incumbent John Quincy Adams by an electoral vote of 178 to 83.

John C. Calhoun later disagreed with Jackson over states rights' issues, and resigned the Vice-Presidency in 1832 after being elected to the Senate.

★ ★ ★

100. **a. fewer voter eligibility requirements.** In our early elections, many states required citizens to own a certain amount of property to qualify to vote. An end to property owning qualifications, supported by followers of Andrew Jackson, contributed to a large voter turnout.

★ ★ ★

101. **a. a "westerner."** A resident of Tennessee, Jackson was the first President to come from the western portion of the United States, as it was then.

The election of 1828 was viewed by many as a victory for the common man. Followers from around the country came to Washington to see Andrew Jackson's inauguration, and many of them proceeded to the White House afterward to celebrate. In the rush – and crush – to see their hero, the crowd ruined many items in the Presidential mansion. Jackson was forced to escape through a back door. The mob was finally coaxed outside when the punch was moved to the White House lawn!

1832

102. Henry Clay of Kentucky was chosen by the National Republicans to face Democratic incumbent Andrew Jackson and his Vice-Presidential candidate Martin van Buren of New York. The election of 1832 featured the first:

    a. front porch campaigns.
    b. debates.
    c. national nominating conventions.
    d. campaign songs.

★   ★   ★

103. At their convention, the Democrats adopted the "two-thirds" rule. What is the "two-thirds" rule?

    a. Two-thirds of the delegates must be present to convene.
    b. Two-thirds of the candidates must be from the North.
    c. A candidate must receive two-thirds of the votes
        in order to win the nomination.
    d. Two-thirds of the delegates must make a speech.

★   ★   ★

104. During the campaign, President Jackson decided to take a strong stand on an issue and wait for the election to see if the voters agreed with him – the first time a President had done so. What was that issue?

    a. His veto of the re-chartering of the Second Bank of the
        United States
    b. A military draft
    c. A federal income tax
    d. A new protectionist tariff

102. **c. national nominating conventions.** The first political convention in the United States was held in September, 1831 by the Anti-Masons, a new third party formed after the disappearance of William Morgan. Morgan had allegedly threatened to publish the secrets of Freemasonry. The Anti-Masons, or Anti-Masonic Party, was formed to counter supposed Masonic influence in government. Their candidate was author and lawyer William Wirt of Maryland. Three months later the National Republicans followed with their own convention, nominating Henry Clay; the Democrats joined in by staging a convention in May of 1832 to re-nominate Andrew Jackson.

★   ★   ★

103. **c. A candidate must receive two-thirds of the votes in order to win the nomination.** The Democrats also passed the "unit rule," which stated that each state must vote as a bloc for the candidate that wins a majority of that state's votes.

★   ★   ★

104. **a. his veto of the re-chartering of the Second Bank of the United States.** Jackson believed the Bank was unconstitutional, inefficient, and that it favored the rich at the expense of everyone else. After the election, he placed federal funds from the Bank in state banks. Re-chartered in Pennsylvania, the Bank failed in 1841, and the United States had no central banking system until the Federal Reserve System was created in 1913. The people agreed with Jackson about the Bank, and reelected him, 219 to 49 electoral votes. Independent Democrat John Floyd of Virginia received all of South Carolina's 11 electoral votes; Vermont's 7 votes went to Anti-Mason William Wirt. A major factor in the election was the use of party newspapers sent around the country by both sides to inform the voters about election issues. The National Republicans' organization didn't compare to the Democrats', who developed superior fundraising techniques and who featured "rallies, barbeques, town meetings, parades, hickory pole raisings and street demonstrations."[32]

1836

105. Henry Clay's defeat by President Jackson signaled the end of the National Republicans. Most of their members joined with conservatives from the North and South to form:

      a. The Whig Party.   **b.** The National Party.
      c. The Freedom Party.   **d.** The Republican Party.

★   ★   ★

106. Vice-President Martin van Buren, Andrew Jackson's hand-picked successor, ran for the Democrats. The Whig Party was not well enough organized to hold a convention. Why did the Whigs run three regional candidates in 1836?

    a. All three candidates were very popular.
    b. They couldn't decide on one candidate.
    c. The candidates had all been loyal supporters
       of the Whig party.
    d. They hoped to take away enough votes from
       van Buren to deny him a majority of electoral votes.

★   ★   ★

107. The election of 1836 marked the first time this important issue played a major role in a campaign:

      a. The tariff   **b.** Immigration
      c. Slavery   **d.** Taxes

1836

105. **a. The Whig Party.** United by their dislike of Andrew Jackson, the Whigs were made up of National Republicans including Henry Clay, who favored internal improvements (road building and other projects) and Democrats such as Daniel Webster, who opposed the expansion of slavery. The Whigs took their name from an English Protestant group of the 1680's who opposed the threat of the establishment of a succession of Catholic kings. The name itself was derived from a Scottish group – the Whigamores.[33] The American Whigs formed their party in opposition to "King Andrew's" use of power, including his use of the veto and the spoils system. Original leaders of the Whig Party included Henry Clay and Daniel Webster.

★ ★ ★

106. **d. They hoped to take away enough votes from van Buren to deny him a majority of electoral votes.** Three regions nominated candidates who were popular in their respective areas: General William Henry Harrison of Ohio, Senator Daniel Webster of Massachusetts, and Hugh Lawson White of Tennessee. The Whigs felt that individually none of their candidates could win, but that three candidates together could keep van Buren from receiving a majority of electoral votes. In that event, the election would go to the House of Representatives, where, hopefully, a Whig President would be chosen. It didn't work. They lost anyway! Referred to as the "Little Magician" because of his political skills, van Buren garnered 170 electoral votes to a combined total of 113 for the others. Independent Willie P. Mangum (undeclared candidate) of North Carolina, received 11 votes. The election of 1836 was the only time a Vice-Presidential candidate did not receive a majority of electoral votes; the Senate decided in favor of former Congressman Richard M. Johnson of Kentucky, 33-16 over Francis Granger of New York.

★ ★ ★

107. **c. Slavery.** By 1836, the abolition of slavery had become a major issue to Americans.

1840

108. The Whigs nominated General William Henry Harrison of Ohio, and, in an effort to attract southern Democratic votes, chose John Tyler, a former Democratic Representative and Senator from Virginia. They challenged Democratic incumbent Martin van Buren and Richard M. Johnson of Kentucky in a campaign that featured:

> **a.** substantive speeches on issues of the day.
> **b.** parades with log cabins and hard cider.
> **c.** the candidates campaigning in every state.
> **d.** the slavery issue.

★   ★   ★

109. Martin van Buren had assorted nicknames, including "Little Van" and "The Little Magician," but following the financial Panic of 1837 and the subsequent depression, opponents of President van Buren referred to him during the campaign of 1840 as:

> **a.** Martin van Depression.   **b.** Martin van Panic.
> **c.** Martin van Broke.   **d.** Martin van Ruin.

★   ★   ★

110. After winning the election of 1840, what was unusual about William Henry Harrison's presidency?

> **a.** He didn't give an inaugural address.
> **b.** He switched parties after being elected.
> **c.** He served the shortest time of any elected President.
> **d.** He didn't live in the White House.

1840

108. **b. parades with log cabins and hard cider.** In 1840, the Whigs were made up of members with opposing views on almost everything! Harrison was told by his advisors not to take a stand on anything or make promises of any kind. Emulating Andrew Jackson's campaigns, he was portrayed as a man of the people and a military hero, living in a humble log cabin. (In fact, he was raised in a well-to-do family and lived in a more-than-comfortable home!) Although his military career was not as distinguished as Jackson's, in 1811, while Governor of the Indiana Territory, Harrison led forces and defeated attacking Indian troops led by the Shawnee Chief Tecumseh near Tippecanoe Creek, earning him the nickname "Old Tippecanoe." In the War of 1812 Harrison defeated British and Indian forces at the Battle of the Thames in Ontario, where Tecumseh was killed. During the campaign of 1840, log cabins were transported in parades through towns and cities, along with barrels of hard cider (a drink as popular as beer is today) for everyone. Parades were said to have been up to ten miles long, with tens of thousands of people singing campaign songs and chanting campaign poems. "Tippecanoe and Tyler Too!" they cheered.[34] "Old Cabin Whiskey" made by E. C. Booz, (whose name endures!) was sold in log cabin shaped bottles, while giant balls 13 feet in diameter (for the 13 original states) were rolled from town to town for Harrison. "Keep the ball rolling!" was the chant.

★ ★ ★

109. **d. Martin van Ruin.** Harrison narrowly won the popular vote, but had a substantial electoral vote margin, 234 to 60. Van Buren didn't even carry New York, his home state.

★ ★ ★

110. **c. He served the shortest time of any elected President.** At 68, Harrison was the oldest man to be elected President up to that time, but after a lengthy inaugural address on a cold, rainy March 4th, he developed pneumonia and lived only one month into his term. John Tyler became the first Vice-President to succeed to the Presidency upon the death of a President.

1844

111. In 1844, Henry Clay ran for President for the third time, this time as a candidate for the Whig Party. For the Democrats, former President Martin van Buren endeavored to win the nomination, but failed to receive enough votes due to the two-third's rule. Incumbent John Tyler wasn't given the nod by the Democrats, and so a "dark horse" candidate was chosen – former Speaker of the House and Governor of Tennessee James K. Polk. During the campaign, Polk advocated the annexation of which future state?

a. Oklahoma   **b.** Texas   **c.** Louisiana   **d.** Mississippi

★ ★ ★

112. Polk favored adding Oregon to the United States clear up to latitude 54°40' – the boundary of Russian held Alaska. What was his slogan regarding Oregon?

a. 54°40' or nothing!   **b.** 54°40' or war!
c. 54°40' or fight!   **d.** 54°40' or else!

★ ★ ★

113. Polk's policy of expansion for the United States was popularly known as:

a. American Destiny.   **b.** Manifest Destiny.
c. Democratic Destiny.   **d.** Polk's Destiny.

1844

111. **b. Texas.** Texas declared its independence from Mexico in 1835. The Mexican War was fought from 1846-48, after which the United States acquired much of the southwest from Mexico, including all or part of California, Nevada, Utah, Wyoming, Colorado and Texas. When Texas entered the Union in 1845, it entered as a slave state.

★　　★　　★

112. **c. 54°40' or fight!** The Oregon Country, including the present-day states of Oregon, Washington, Idaho and parts of Wyoming, Montana and Canadian British Columbia, had been jointly held by the Americans and the British since 1818. Both sides had become unhappy with joint ownership. The Americans wanted the Oregon Country to become part of the United States all the way up to Alaska. After peaceful negotiations between the two countries, the Oregon Treaty of 1846 established the northwestern border of the United States at the 49th parallel. The area north of that became British Columbia, now part of Canada.

Polk defeated Clay, 170 to 105 electoral votes. Because anti-slavery Whigs in New York State voted for abolitionist James G. Birney of the Liberty Party, Clay lost New York. If he had won there, Clay would have won the election. However, not all of Polk's votes were obtained legally. In large cities, campaign workers arranged for immigrants to register illegally – to vote for Polk. And people were taken by boat up and down the Mississippi River – voting for Polk in each town![35]

★　　★　　★

113. **b. Manifest Destiny.** Manifest Destiny was the term used to justify belief in American expansion throughout North America.

1848

114. President Polk had had enough of the trials and tribulations of the Presidency. He had won the Mexican War, negotiated the peaceful surrender of New Mexico and California from Mexico, settled the Oregon boundary dispute peacefully, and was now more than happy to leave the White House. The Democrats turned to Senator Lewis Cass of Michigan to face Whig candidate General Zachary Taylor of Louisiana. Taylor was well-known as a hero of:

      a. The Mexican War.   **b.** The Texas War.
      c. The War of 1812.   **d.** The Revolutionary War.

★   ★   ★

115. Former President Martin van Buren ran as the candidate of the Free Soil Party. What was the Free Soil Party?

      a. A pro-slavery party
      b. An anti-slavery party
      c. A party that favored free land for immigrants
      d. A party that built log cabins for free

★   ★   ★

116. Taylor's candidacy was supported by his former son-in-law, Jefferson Davis. Davis held several government positions. For which of these offices is he most well-known?

      a. Congressman from Mississippi
      b. Senator from Mississippi
      c. President of the Confederate States of America
      d. Secretary of War in the Pierce administration

114. **a. The Mexican War.** A professional soldier, Taylor moved frequently and never had a permanent residence. He never voted before 1848, claiming that as a career soldier, he didn't want to be put in the position of possibly voting against a future commander in chief.[36] Along with his Vice-Presidential candidate, former Congressman Millard Fillmore of New York, Taylor won, 163 to 127 electoral votes.

★   ★   ★

115. **b. An anti-slavery party.** The Free Soilers opposed the expansion of slavery into the new territories, with the hope that homesteaders could move to those lands without competition from wealthy large-scale slave owners. The Wilmot Proviso, a bill to ban slavery from territories acquired during the Mexican War, dominated the campaign. Taylor, the owner of more than 100 slaves, didn't comment directly on the issue of slavery. Democrat Cass opposed it, proposing that new territories decide the issue of slavery for themselves.[37] Although van Buren received no electoral votes, he split the Democratic vote in New York, giving the state and the election to Zachary Taylor.

★   ★   ★

116. **c. President of the Confederate States of America.** Elected to Congress in 1845, Jefferson Davis resigned to fight in the Mexican War, and subsequently took over the management of a plantation in Mississippi. A United States Senator from 1847 to 1861, he resigned his seat and returned to Mississippi to consider secession with fellow members of the Mississippi congressional delegation. As a Senator, he had originally opposed secession, but went along with his delegation's decision to secede from the Union. In 1861 Davis began a six-year term as President of the Confederacy. Captured by Union troops on May 10, 1865, he was charged with treason, and spent two years in prison.

Davis served as Secretary of War in the Franklin Pierce administration from 1853-57, and "modernized the army that . . . ironically, a decade later would crush the rebellion Davis led as President of the Confederate States of America."[38]

1852

117. President Taylor died in office – from either sunstroke or from eating a bowl of spoiled cherries and milk at a July 4th celebration in 1850. Vice-President Millard Fillmore completed Taylor's term as President but did not receive the Democratic nomination in 1852. Another "dark horse" candidate – former Senator Franklin Pierce of New Hampshire – was chosen. How many ballots did it take to agree to his nomination?

a. 25   **b.** 30   **c.** 37   **d.** 49

★   ★   ★

118. Pierce was opposed by Whig candidate and Mexican War hero General Winfield Scott of New Jersey. Both party platforms endorsed compromise legislation that included the admission of California to the Union as a free state, and the Fugitive Slave Act. What was the name of this legislation?

> **a.** The California Compromise
> **b.** The Slave Act Compromise
> **c.** The Compromise of 1850
> **d.** The North-South Compromise

★   ★   ★

119. Franklin Pierce was considered a "doughface." What was a "doughface?"

> **a.** A politician who switched parties
> **b.** A northern Democrat with Southern sympathies
> **c.** A southern Democrat who sided with the North
> **d.** A politician who ate a lot of pastry

117. **d. 49.** None of the four major candidates was able to capture the required two-third's votes at the convention. The lead changed hands several times, while supporters of Franklin Pierce awaited the right moment to present him as a viable candidate. Nominated by Virginia, he was voted in on the 49th ballot. Southerners felt that Pierce, a northern Democrat, was open minded regarding the expansion of slavery, and since he hadn't taken a stand on most issues, was acceptable as a compromise candidate to the other delegates.

★   ★   ★

118. **c. The Compromise of 1850.** Intended by Henry Clay to settle the issue of slavery and to avert Civil War, the Compromise of 1850 admitted California as a free state, defined the borders of Texas, established the territories of Utah and New Mexico, and gave Texas $10 million to pay off its debts. It also enacted the Fugitive Slave Act, which required fugitive slaves to be returned to their masters - with help from the government if necessary. Many southern slaveholders claimed free northern blacks as their runaway slaves, illegally returning them to slavery in the South. The Compromise also abolished the slave trade in the District of Columbia, although the institution of slavery was allowed to continue there.[39]

★   ★   ★

119. **b. A northern Democrat with southern sympathies.** Used to describe northern Congressmen, especially Democrats who went along with the expansion of slavery, the term "doughface" was originally used to describe a leader who would not stand up to strong opposition. He would not "set his jaw" against his opponent, but would be pliable - like dough - and would agree with him in order to reach a compromise.[40] Northern Democrats who supported the Missouri Compromise, or who believed that the federal government should let residents in the territories acquired in the Mexican War decide the issue of slavery for themselves, were referred to as "doughfaces." Pierce defeated Scott, 254 to 42 electoral votes.

1856

120. Ex-President Millard Fillmore ran for the American, or Know-Nothing Party. What was the Know-Nothing Party?

    a. A party whose members, when asked what they stood for, replied: "I know nothing."
    b. A party whose members claimed they knew nothing about politics
    c. A party whose members didn't want to take a stand on the issue of slavery
    d. A party whose members never went to school

★ ★ ★

121. Disagreement over the issue of slavery finally broke up the Whig party. A new party was formed by northern Whigs, anti-slavery Democrats and Free Soilers. What was the name of this party?

    a. The Union Party   **b.** The American Party
    c. The Barnburner Party   **d.** The Republican Party

★ ★ ★

122. The Democrats nominated former Congressman and Secretary of State James Buchanan of Pennsylvania. His opponent – the first Republican Presidential candidate – was:

    a. John C. Fremont   **b.** Abraham Lincoln
    c. Ulysses S. Grant   **d.** Henry Clay

★★★ *THE ELECTIONS★ANSWERS* ★★★
1856

120. **a. A party whose members, when asked what they stood for, replied: "I know nothing."** Organized in 1852, the Know-Nothing Party favored stricter immigration laws in response to increased Irish immigration in the East and German immigration in the Midwest. Feeling threatened economically and politically by the newcomers, they met in secret, refusing to voice their beliefs. With increasing membership, they eventually shed their secretive ways, and became known as the "American Party." Know-Nothings had 43 members in the House and five in the Senate in 1855. Although their presidential candidate Millard Fillmore received 21% of the popular vote in 1856, the party eventually split on the issue of slavery, and lost its support by the end of the decade. ★ ★ ★

121. **d. The Republican Party.** Founded in 1854 by "conscience" Whigs, Free Soilers and anti-slavery Democrats, the Republican Party held its first convention in Philadelphia in June, 1856. They viewed slavery as a great moral, social and political evil. Opposed to the spread of slavery in the territories, some of their support came from Western farmers who didn't want competition from slaveholders in the Western territories, and from Eastern businessmen who felt that if slavery were to spread to the territories, a majority in Congress would eventually be sympathetic to southern causes, thus blocking legislation favorable to eastern states. ★ ★ ★

122. **a. John C. Fremont.** A national hero known for exploring the West, Fremont had no political record to defend and was acceptable to all factions of the Republican Party. He lost to James Buchanan, 174 to 114 electoral votes, but made a good showing, as the Republicans were viewed as a third party to the Democrats and the Whigs. Most of Fremont's support came from the North. Know-Nothing candidate Martin van Buren received eight electoral votes – all from the state of Maryland. James Buchanan was the third of three "doughface" Presidents, after Fillmore and Pierce. Cried the Republicans: "Free Speech, Free Press, Free Soil, Free Men, Fremont and Victory!"[41]

1860

123. The young Republican Party nominated former Illinois Congressman Abraham Lincoln for President and Hannibal Hamlin of Maine for Vice-President. There were four major Presidential candidates in 1860. One of Lincoln's opponents was the same Democrat he had faced unsuccessfully two years earlier in the Illinois race for the U.S. Senate. Who was that candidate?

a. Benjamin Harrison   **b.** William H. Herndon
c. Stephen A. Douglas   **d.** Daniel Webster

★ ★ ★

124. Slavery was the main issue in 1860, but it was closely related to what other issue?

a. Immigration   **b.** Taxes
c. States' rights   **d.** Education

★ ★ ★

125. Following the election of 1860, what did seven of the nine slave states do?

a. Secede from the Union
b. Form the Confederate States of America
c. Appoint a President of the Confederacy
d. All of the above

1860

123. **c. Stephen A. Douglas.** Advocating "popular sovereignty," (allowing each territory to decide the slavery issue for itself) Douglas won the Illinois Senate race. However, Lincoln became nationally known for questioning the morality of slavery during their seven debates in 1858. Small in stature, Douglas was called "the little giant" for his eloquent defense of "popular sovereignty." ★ ★ ★

124. **c. States' rights.** The South opposed popular sovereignty for the territories on the issue of slavery. If territories entered the Union as free states, the South would be outnumbered and its influence in Congress regarding slavery would be diminished. Lincoln stayed home in Springfield, Illinois during the campaign; his name didn't even appear on the ballot in most southern states. Stephen Douglas traveled the country, predicting secession if Lincoln won. With 47% of the popular vote, the Democrats split their vote between moderate Douglas and pro-slavery candidate John Breckenridge, (nominated by southern Democrats favoring federal protection of slavery). John Bell of Tennessee of the Constitutional Union Party (pledged to maintain the Union) carried three states. Lincoln received 40% of the popular vote and 180 electoral votes; Breckenridge had 72 electoral votes, Bell: 39 and Douglas: 12. ★ ★ ★

125. **d. All of the above.** South Carolina was the first to secede, on December 20, 1860. By February, 1861, six other states: Florida, Mississippi, Alabama, Georgia, Louisiana and Texas had joined them. On February 4, 1861 they declared their union with the United States dissolved and on February 8th formed the Confederate States of America. After the start of the Civil War in April, 1861 they were joined by Virginia, Arkansas, North Carolina and Tennessee. The South had threatened to secede so many times that many people didn't take its threats seriously. Four slave states - Delaware, Maryland, Kentucky and Missouri – stayed in the Union; Kentucky and Missouri were represented by two of the stars on the Confederate flag.

1864

126. Why did Lincoln and the Republicans replace Vice-President Hannibal Hamlin of Maine with Southern Democrat Andrew Johnson of Tennessee for the campaign of 1864?

    a. Hamlin didn't want to run again.
    b. Hamlin didn't get along with Lincoln.
    c. Hamlin favored slavery.
    d. Johnson had remained loyal to the Union.

★ ★ ★

127. Democratic candidate General George B. McClellan of New York, whom Lincoln had fired from his duties as general earlier in the Civil War, challenged the President. Why did Abraham Lincoln feel he would not be reelected in 1864?

    a. He felt he was too old.
    b. He felt he wasn't a good speaker.
    c. The Civil War hadn't ended.
    d. He hadn't campaigned.

★ ★ ★

128. Some thought the election should have been postponed or suspended because of the Civil War. How was the election carried out?

    a. The same as in peacetime
    b. The date was delayed.
    c. The date was moved up.
    d. There were riots and protests at the polling places.

1864

126. **d. Johnson had remained loyal to the Union.** And the Republicans felt it would improve Lincoln's chances of winning with a Southerner on the ticket. A former Democratic Senator from Tennessee, Johnson had been appointed military governor of Tennessee in 1862 by Abraham Lincoln. Johnson had been the only southern Senator to remain in Congress when the South seceded. He favored the Union, and tried in vain to keep Tennessee from seceding. As a "War Democrat," it was believed that Johnson would attract votes from Southern Democrats who favored the war. In the North, Johnson was regarded as a hero; in the South, a traitor. At the Republican convention, Hamlin lost the Vice-Presidential nomination to Johnson, 200 to 150 votes.

In an effort to accommodate Democrats who supported the Union war effort, the Republicans called themselves the National Union Party.[42]

★ ★ ★

127. **c. The Civil War hadn't ended.** Lincoln's opponent, General George B. McClellan, had been replaced by Lincoln during the war for his failure to pursue the retreating army of Robert E. Lee after the Battle of Antietam in September, 1862. McClellan was favored to win at the outset of the campaign. However, just when Lincoln had lost almost all hope of winning, the Union Army achieved major gains, and the Democrats' platform of an immediate armistice became a liability.

★ ★ ★

128. **a. The same as in peacetime.** Lincoln himself noted the "extraordinary calmness and good order with which the millions of voters met and mingled at the polls" and that "a people's government can sustain a national election in the midst of a civil war."[43] Said Lincoln: "We cannot have free government without election, and if the rebellion could force us to forgo, or postpone a national election, it might fairly claim to have already conquered and ruined us."[44]

1864

129. What was the attitude of the opposition press toward Lincoln during the campaign?

    a. They gave him overwhelming support because of the war.
    b. The press didn't take sides during the Civil War.
    c. Lincoln's personality and conduct of the war. were attacked by the opposition press.
    d. The press generally avoided criticism of the President during the Civil War.

★   ★   ★

130. What was Lincoln's attitude toward the attacks hurled at him during the election?

    a. He ignored them.
    b. He laughed at them.
    c. He was upset that he was always involved in elections marked by bitterness.
    d. He decided not to read the newspapers anymore.

★   ★   ★

131. The capture of which southern city helped Lincoln win reelection in 1864?

    a. Richmond   **b.** Nashville   **c.** Savannah   **d.** Atlanta

129. **c. Lincoln's personality and conduct of the war were attacked by the opposition press.** The press took sides during the Civil War, and did not hesitate to include the President in its attacks. Lincoln was criticized on many counts, including curbing civil liberties, and was the victim of some nasty name-calling. Said the *New York World:* "The age of statesmen is gone; the age of railsplitters and tailors, of buffoons, boors and fanatics has succeeded."[45] *Harper's* listed attacks on Lincoln: "Filthy Story Teller, Despot, Liar, Thief, Braggart, Buffoon, Usurper, Monster, Ignoramus Abe, Old Scoundrel, Perjurer, Robber, Swindler, Tyrant, Fiend, Butcher" – attributed to friends of his opponent.[46]

★   ★   ★

130. **c. He was upset that he was always involved in elections marked by bitterness.** "It is a little singular that I, who am not a vindictive man... should have always been before the people for election in canvasses marked for their bitterness..."[47] Said the *New York Herald*: "His election was a very sorry joke. The idea that such a man as he should be President of such a country as this is a very ridiculous joke...His inaugural address was a joke...His emancipation proclamation was a solemn joke...His conversation is full of jokes...His title of 'Honest' is a satirical joke...His intrigues to secure a re-nomination and the hopes he appears to entertain of a reelection are, however, the most laughable jokes of all."[48]

However, Lincoln remained very popular - in the North - with the people.

★   ★   ★

131. **d. Atlanta.** The successes of the Union Army during the summer and fall of 1864, particularly the capture of Atlanta by General William Tecumseh Sherman, helped secure a victory for Lincoln. The Union soldiers were allowed to vote, and supported Lincoln overwhelmingly. Lincoln won, 212 to 21 electoral votes.

1868

132. Vice-President Andrew Johnson became President upon the assassination of Abraham Lincoln in April, 1865, just as the Civil War was coming to a close. A major reason that Johnson, a Democrat, was not chosen by his party to run for President in his own right in 1868 was that:

> **a.** he was a southerner.
> **b.** there had been an impeachment trial against him in 1868.
> **c.** he wasn't a good campaigner.
> **d.** he favored harsh treatment of southern states returning to the Union.

★   ★   ★

133. Republican Ulysses S. Grant of Illinois faced Democrat Horatio Seymour, former Governor of New York. What was Grant's main attraction as a candidate?

> **a.** His time spent on the campaign trail
> **b.** His popularity as a politician
> **c.** His popularity as a war hero
> **d.** His speaking ability

★   ★   ★

134. The main issue of the campaign of 1868 was:

> **a.** Retribution   **c.** Foreign Policy
> **b.** Territorial expansion   **d.** Reconstruction

132. **b. there had been an impeachment trial against him in 1868.** Facing strong resistance from Republicans in Congress regarding his leniency toward the South after the war, Johnson vetoed twenty-nine pieces of legislation, fifteen of which were overridden by Congress. In February, 1868, in defiance of the Tenure of Office Act (which forbade removal of Senate-confirmed federal officials without the Senate's consent) Johnson fired Secretary of War Edwin Stanton, who opposed his policies. The House then voted 126 to 47 to impeach the President for "high crimes and misdemeanors." Most of the eleven articles brought against Johnson involved his alleged violation of the Office of Tenure Act. Johnson was acquitted by the Senate by a vote of 35 to 19, one vote short of the two-thirds needed for conviction and removal from office. Seven Republican Senators joined Democrats in voting for acquittal. Although the articles of impeachment stated that Johnson "did attempt to bring into disgrace, ridicule, hatred, contempt and reproach the Congress" many Republicans felt that his behavior as President did not warrant impeachment, and in addition, were opposed to the succession of Benjamin Wade of Ohio, who, as President Pro Tempore of the Senate, would have been next in line in Presidential succession. ★ ★ ★

133. **c. His popularity as a war hero.** When Grant suffered setbacks during the Civil war, it was suggested that Lincoln fire him. Lincoln refused, answering: "I can't spare this man - he fights!"[49] Upon signing his letter of acceptance for the Republican Presidential nomination, Grant added: "Let us have peace." The phrase became a campaign slogan.[50] He won by a small popular vote margin, but the electoral vote was 214 to 80.

★ ★ ★

134. **d. Reconstruction.** After the Civil War, the Confederate states rejoined the Union during the period known as Reconstruction. Union troops were stationed in every southern state - except Andrew Johnson's home state of Tennessee – until Reconstruction ended in 1877.

1872

135. Many Republicans didn't support the re-nomination of President Grant. They called for reform of the civil service, an end to Reconstruction including withdrawal of federal troops from the South, and "equal justice for all." What did this group of reformers call themselves?

    a. Moderate Republicans   **b.** New Republicans
    c. Anti-Grant Republicans   **d.** Liberal Republicans

★ ★ ★

136. Defeating a challenge from Charles Francis Adams, son of John Quincy Adams, New York Times editor Horace Greeley was supported by Liberal Republicans. Who did the Democrats support?

    a. Grover Cleveland   **b.** Horace Greeley
    c. Susan B. Anthony   **d.** Charles Francis Adams

★ ★ ★

137. With the Fifteenth Amendment to the Constitution (1870) African-Americans were guaranteed the right to vote. However, in 1872 women did not have the right to vote in many states, including New York. Suffragette Susan B. Anthony voted anyway – in Rochester on November 5th. What happened after that?

    a. She was arrested.
    b. She gave up her campaign for women's suffrage.
    c. She wrote to President Grant.
    d. She became a lawyer.

1872

135. **d. Liberal Republicans.** They were displeased with the scandals and corruption of the Grant administration, and favored leniency for the South after the Civil War. The Liberal Republican Party was short-lived; most of its members joined the Democratic Party after the election of 1872.

★ ★ ★

136. **b. Horace Greeley.** The same candidate as the Liberal Republicans! Even though Greeley had criticized their party for years, Democrats decided to support him for President. "Anyone but Grant!" they cried. The election was unusual: the Republican incumbent, Grant, was a former Democrat; and Greeley, endorsed by the Liberals and Democrats, had attacked liberal policies and was a founder of the Republican Party.[51] Greeley was mercilessly attacked in the press; his opponents pointed out that his ideas, ranging from free trade to free love, were too radical for the country.[52] Saddened by the death of his wife shortly before the election, and disheartened by his loss at the polls, he died soon after the election. When the electoral votes were counted, Grant won reelection, 286 to 66. Greeley's electors split their votes among several candidates, but three electors voted for him anyway. Congress didn't count them.

★ ★ ★

137. **a. She was arrested.** On November 18, 1872, Susan B. Anthony was arrested for voting on November 5th. The presiding judge at her trial, Associate Supreme Court Justice Ward Hunt, refused to let her testify, permitted Anthony's testimony after being arrested to be admitted into the record, wrote his opinion before the trial, instructed the jury to deliver a verdict of "guilty," and refused to let the jury be polled. A motion for a new trial was refused. After lecturing the judge on his violation of her rights, and after she was fined $100 - plus the costs of the prosecution - Anthony told the judge: "I will never pay a dollar of your unjust penalty!"[53]

And she didn't!

1876

138. The Democrats nominated Governor Samuel J. Tilden of New York, a well-known reformer who had sent New York City Democratic boss William Marcy Tweed to jail. Grant's administration had been plagued by major financial scandals (not involving him). Hoping for nomination for a third term, he apologized to the nation for the scandals, but Republicans instead nominated Ohio Governor Rutherford B. Hayes. What was unusual about this election?

    a. The election results were disputed.
    b. Very few voters went to the polls.
    c. It was a huge landslide for Hayes.
    d. There weren't enough volunteers to count the votes.

★ ·★ ★

139. The election of 1876 was decided by:

    a. the House of Representatives.
    b. the Senate.
    c. the Supreme Court.
    d. a special electoral commission.

★ ★ ★

140. After the election was decided, the two parties agreed to a deal that came to be known as the Great Compromise. What did this involve?

    a. New voting procedures   **b.** Civil service reform
    c. The end of Reconstruction   **d.** The vote for women

1876

138. **a. The election results were disputed.** The morning after the election, Samuel J. Tilden had 184 electoral votes, one short of a majority, to 165 for Hayes. However, twenty more votes were in doubt: seven in South Carolina, eight in Louisiana, four in Florida and one of Oregon's three votes. There was fraud on both sides in the three southern states in question. Eventually, two sets of results were sent to the Electoral College from Louisiana and South Carolina - one for Tilden and one for Hayes – and three sets from Florida, two for Tilden and one for Hayes.

★ ★ ★

139. **d. a special electoral commission.** The Constitution does not provide for settlement of disputed votes. The House was controlled by Democrats, the Senate by Republicans. After weeks of debate, Congress agreed upon a special electoral commission of five Senators, five Representatives and five Supreme Court Justices – eight Republicans to seven Democrats. The eighth Republican, Justice Joseph Bradley, (a replacement appointee to the commission) was expected to be non-partisan. He wasn't, and voted with the other Republicans on every important issue. On March 2, 1877, by an 8 to 7 vote, the commission gave all of the disputed electoral votes to Hayes, and with them, the Presidency. The final electoral vote was Hayes: 185, Tilden: 184. The popular vote was Tilden: 51%, Hayes: 48%. Greenback candidate Peter Cooper received 1% of the vote.

★ ★ ★

140. **c. The end of Reconstruction.** The Democrats agreed not to contest the results of the electoral commission. In return, the Republicans agreed to the end of Reconstruction in the South, withdrawing all remaining federal troops from the southern states.

1880

141. Upon his acceptance of the Presidential nomination in 1876, Hayes promised to serve only one term. After four years in office, his popularity had waned and he was happy to retire. Why had he become unpopular?

    a. For raising taxes
    b. For his foreign policy
    c. For crushing the 1877 railroad strike
    d. For spending too much time on vacation

★ ★ ★

142. The Democrats nominated Civil War General Winfield Scott Hancock, who had no political experience. During the campaign, Republicans printed a pamphlet about him entitled "A Record of the Statesmanship and Political Achievements of General Winfield Scott Hancock...Compiled from the Records." What was in this pamphlet?

    a. Poems deriding Hancock
    b. Cartoons of Hancock
    c. Hancock's few political achievements
    d. Blank pages

★ ★ ★

143. Republican Ulysses S. Grant, out of office since 1877, lost his bid for re-nomination for an unprecedented third term. Instead, the Republicans turned to "dark horse" James A. Garfield, Congressman from Ohio, with Chester A. Arthur, former collector (of duties) of the Port of New York, for Vice-President. The Presidential candidates agreed on many things, including this issue that would lead to tragedy for James Garfield:

    a. Civil Service reform   **b.** The tariff
    c. Taxes   **d.** Immigration

1880

141. **c. For crushing the 1877 railroad strike.** On July 2, 1877, the Baltimore & Ohio Railroad announced its third wage cut in three years, which resulted in striking workers. Riots broke out in several cities and much of the railroad service in the country was halted. President Hayes sent troops to five states to prevent interference with the trains. For this he was very unpopular.

★   ★   ★

142. **d. Blank pages.** Hancock did no campaigning. Garfield conducted a front porch campaign, giving speeches at his home in Mentor, Ohio, just outside of Cleveland.

★   ★   ★

143. **a. Civil Service reform.** Since the time of Andrew Jackson, winning candidates had awarded government jobs to members of their own political party in what was known as the "spoils system." However, this meant that there were new appointments with every change of President. Some positions required specialized skills, but qualified workers would not apply for jobs they might lose in four years. In addition, the change of employees every four years led to waste and confusion. The problem became serious, as each new President and other officials were deluged by office seekers.

Garfield received a popular vote margin of just a few thousand votes, but won the election, 214 to 155 electoral votes. However, in July, 1881, a deranged office seeker who had been turned down for a government position shot Garfield at a Washington D.C. railroad station. The President died two months later. This tragic turn of events finally led to civil service reform, which put an end to political appointments for many government jobs, and required applicants to pass exams before being hired.[54]

1884

144. The campaign of 1884 featured Republican James G. Blaine of Maine and Democrat Grover Cleveland, Governor of New York and former mayor of Buffalo. At the Democratic convention in Chicago, Cleveland was the front runner. His only opposition came from a famous political machine which was called:

> **a.** The Muckrakers. **b.** Tammany Hall.
> **c.** The Half-Breeds. **d.** The Stalwarts.

★ ★ ★

145. Some Republicans switched their support from Blaine to Democrat Grover Cleveland. They were known as:

> **a.** Clevelanders. **b.** Republicrats.
> **c.** Traitors. **d.** Mugwumps.

★ ★ ★

146. With the campaign focusing on the personal character of the candidates more than the issues, "Slippery Jim" Blaine was attacked for profiting from his connections with railroad interests as a Congressman. For what was Cleveland attacked?

a. Appointing friends to office while governor of New York
b. Taking bribes while governor
c. Having fathered an illegitimate child
d. Favoring big business

144. **b. Tammany Hall.** Founded in New York in 1786, the Tammany Society was organized to benefit Revolutionary War veterans and their families. Named after the Delaware chief Tammanend, it evolved into a powerful political machine in New York, granting favors in exchange for votes, and influencing elections. New immigrants were given assistance by Tammany Hall, and then expected to vote for Tammany candidates at elections. Extremely powerful in the mid-19th century in both Tammany Hall and the Democratic Party, Boss William Marcy Tweed became highly corrupt. Along with his cronies he defrauded New York City of at least $30 million. Convicted on 204 counts, he escaped from jail twice; he died in a U.S. prison in 1876.[55] ★ ★ ★

145. **d. Mugwumps.** Originally an Algonquin word meaning "chief," the term mugwump refers to "any independent, especially in politics."[56] It was used in 1884 to characterize Republicans who supported Cleveland instead of Blaine for President. A former Speaker of the House and twice Secretary of State, Blaine lost the support of many Republicans due to allegations that he exchanged political favors for railroad stock as a member of Congress. ★ ★ ★

146. **c. Having fathered an illegitimate child.** Grover Cleveland was known for his moral character, honesty and efficiency while mayor of Buffalo, N.Y. When confronted with charges of having fathered an illegitimate child as a young man, he advised his handlers to tell the truth. "A Terrible Tale – Dark Chapter in a Public Man's History" read the headline in the *Buffalo Evening Telegraph.* Cleveland wasn't totally certain he was the father, but agreed to accept responsibility for child support. A bachelor at the time, he felt he had the least to lose compared to the other potential – married - fathers! Cried the Republicans: "Ma, Ma, where's my Pa?" Replied the Democrats: "Gone to the White House, Ha ,Ha, Ha!"[57]

Cleveland won, 219 to 182 electoral votes.

1888

147. Which of the following was new and different for the election of 1888?

      a. Write-in voting   **b.** All new polling places
      c. Secret ballots   **d.** Hanging chads

★   ★   ★

148. President Grover Cleveland was challenged by Republican Benjamin Harrison. The main issue for the voters in 1888 was:

      a. the tariff.   **b.** the gold standard.
      c. immigration.   **d.** imperialism.

★   ★   ★

149. Grover Cleveland won the popular vote, but failed to win the electoral vote. He would have won the election if he had won this state:

      a. His Vice-Presidential candidate's home state, Ohio
      b. His home state, New York
      c. California
      d. Pennsylvania

1888

147. c. Secret ballots. However, widespread vote-buying made this election one of the most corrupt ever.[58]

Initially used in Australia, the secret or "Australian" ballot made its first appearance in the United States in Kentucky in 1888, and by 1892, 33 states were using it. Over the years significant problems had arisen with the use of the ballot box, with some candidates having to pay outrageous sums to be put on the ballot. Voters could be bribed and intimidated.[59] Ballots were often printed by the parties, with each party using a different color of paper. The election judges could see how a person voted. When the voting laws outlawed colored paper, the parties used paper with different textures, and judges could "feel" who voted for which candidates![60] By 1910, the Australian ballot was in wide use in the United States, and the voting laws established in the 1880's and 1890's employing the secret ballot are basically those that we use today.[61]

★ ★ ★

148. a. the tariff. Cleveland and the Democrats proposed a reduction in the tariff, while Harrison and the Republicans favored a protective tariff. There were few issues dividing the candidates, and party organization in getting out the vote probably made the difference for the Republicans.[62]

★ ★ ★

149. b. His home state, New York. Cleveland would have won reelection if he had carried his home state, New York. His opposition to the political machine, Tammany Hall, was a factor in his defeat in New York. Since Cleveland opposed their tactics of exchanging political favors, and had worked against corruption, Tammany Hall refused to campaign for him. In addition, Cleveland's veto of Civil War veterans' pension benefits and his opposition to drought relief for farmers eroded his support. New York's 36 electoral votes would have put him over the top. Cleveland narrowly won the popular vote, 49% to 48%, but lost the electoral vote to Harrison, 233 to 168.

1892

150. Former President Grover Cleveland challenged incumbent Benjamin Harrison. What unusual statement did Cleveland's wife make to the staff when they left the White House after losing the election of 1888?

> **a.** "This place is no fun to live in."
> **b.** "We're glad to leave the White House."
> **c.** "We'll miss the White House."
> **d.** "We'll be back in four years!"

★ ★ ★

151. A new political group representing the farmers and workers was very active in the campaign of 1892. They called themselves the:

> **a.** Populists.   **b.** Farmer-Labor Party.
> **c.** Silverites.   **d.** Laborites.

★ ★ ★

152. An effective campaigner, Democratic Vice-Presidential nominee Adlai Stevenson spoke to voters across the country in 1892. One issue of importance to residents in Washington State was:

> **a.** gold mining.
> **b.** international shipping.
> **c.** striking workers.
> **d.** naming the great mountain there "Rainier" or "Tacoma."

1892

150. d. "We'll be back in four years!" And they were!" With a victory in 1892, Cleveland became the only President to be elected to two non-consecutive terms.

Grover Cleveland was the only President to be married in the White House. In 1886 he married Frances Folsom; he was 49, she was 21.

★   ★   ★

151. a. Populists. Calling themselves the Peoples' Party, the Populists chose James B. Weaver of Iowa as their Presidential candidate; Weaver had run in 1880 as a candidate of the Greenback Labor Party (favoring large amounts of paper money in circulation). With an expanding world market in agriculture after the Civil War, prices for wheat, cotton and other exports had declined. Farmers wanted higher prices for their produce; they needed more money to pay for their expensive farm equipment, for which they had mortgaged their farms at high interest rates. The Populists favored the unlimited coinage of silver and an increase of paper money in circulation to inflate the currency. They also reflected deep concerns in the country regarding corporate influence in American politics. Cleveland and other fiscal conservatives felt the "free silver plank" would threaten the American economic order.[63] Weaver received over one million popular votes in 1892, and carried four states with 22 electoral votes – a strong showing for a young third party. Cleveland won 277 votes; Harrison, 145.

★   ★   ★

152. d. naming the great mountain there "Rainier" or "Tacoma." Standing at the rear platform of his train, Stevenson would proclaim the beauty of the mountain and would end with: "...I pledge myself here and now that if elected I will not rest until this glorious mountain is properly named..." – at which point he would pull on a secret cord. The engineer would blow the whistle and, together with a blast of steam, drown out Stevenson's last words as the trained pulled out![64]

1896

153. Republican William McKinley, Governor and former Congressman from Ohio, was opposed by the editor of the *Omaha World-Herald*, former Democratic Congressman from Nebraska William Jennings Bryan. The main issue of the campaign was:

> **a.** labor unions.
> **b.** independence for Cuba.
> **c.** the gold standard vs. the free coinage of silver.
> **d.** American imperialism.

★   ★   ★

154. William Jennings Bryan was known as a great orator. In 1896 he traveled 18,000 miles and spoke to millions of Americans. What did William McKinley do to counter Bryan's campaign style?

> **a.** He traveled over 20,000 miles.
> **b.** He went to every state in the country.
> **c.** He spoke in all the major cities.
> **d.** He conducted a front porch campaign from his home in Canton, Ohio.

★   ★   ★

155. McKinley's campaign was run by wealthy Cleveland industrialist Mark Hanna. This was the first campaign to:

> **a.** use systematic fundraising techniques.
> **b.** sing campaign songs.
> **c.** make use of radio.
> **d.** hold rallies.

153. **c. The gold standard vs. the free coinage of silver.** The Panic of 1893 had touched off a serious depression. Unemployment was high, many banks had been forced to close and farm prices had dropped sharply. Representing the Populists and the Democrats, Bryan – dubbed a "Popocrat" – promoted the idea of "free silver," advocating the unlimited coinage of silver at a rate of sixteen ounces of silver to one ounce of gold in order to "raise prices, lift the crushing burden of debt, and restore prosperity."[65] McKinley and the Republicans, seen as supporters of the wealthy, favored the gold standard, whereby paper money can be converted to gold and the value of currency is based on the value of gold. Attacking those who would exploit the poor, Bryan proclaimed at the Democratic convention: "You shall not press down upon the brow of labor this crown of thorns, you shall not crucify mankind upon a cross of gold!"[66]   ★   ★   ★

154. **d. He conducted a front porch campaign from his home in Canton, Ohio.** McKinley felt he couldn't outdo Bryan at his own game. Delegations were brought to his home in Canton, Ohio daily, where prepared questions and answers were exchanged as he advocated higher protective tariffs to cure the nation's economic woes. Although Grover Cleveland and the Democrats weren't responsible for the depression, they were back in power in 1893, and received the blame for it. Now the tide was turning in favor of the Republicans. Bryan carried the South, the Plains and the Mountain states, but McKinley won, 271 to 176 electoral votes, carrying the industrial North and Midwest, and several states in the West. Republicans successfully portrayed Bryan as a radical, but the way was paved for broad economic and social reforms.   ★   ★   ★

155. **a. use systematic fundraising techniques.** Led by Hanna, the Republicans raised and spent over $3.5 million; Bryan raised a fraction of that. Hundreds of supporters toured the country delivering the Republican message for McKinley, while tens of millions of pieces of campaign literature were distributed.

1900

156. William Jennings Bryan launched his second campaign against William McKinley, now the incumbent. Vice-President Garret A. Hobart of New Jersey had died in office. Why did New York Republican political boss Thomas Platt work quietly behind the scenes to promote Governor Theodore Roosevelt of New York for Vice-President it 1900?

  a. He thought Roosevelt would be a great Vice-President.
  b. He liked Roosevelt's record as Governor of New York.
  c. He thought a Roosevelt Vice-Presidency would be helpful to New York.
  d. He wanted Roosevelt out of New York because he was too hard to control.

★　★　★

157. With the acquisition of islands in the Caribbean and the Pacific, what became a central issue of the campaign of 1900?

  a. International trade　　**b.** American imperialism
  c. Foreign policy　　**d.** Immigration from those islands

★　★　★

158. The issue that ultimately made the difference in McKinley's reelection was:

  a. imperialism.　　**b.** renewed prosperity at home.
  c. large voter turnout.　　**d.** the Spanish-American War.

156. **d. He wanted Roosevelt out of New York because he was too hard to control.** Roosevelt - already famous for his adventures as a cowboy out West, for leading the Rough Riders in Cuba during the Spanish-American War, as Police Commissioner of New York City and as Governor of New York - was strongly favored by many at the Republican convention for Vice-President. Boss Platt saw this as a chance to get rid of the independent minded Roosevelt, whom he couldn't control. Fearing the Vice-Presidency would be a dead-end politically, Roosevelt denied interest in the nomination, but enjoyed the attention! "We want Teddy!" was the cry. By the convention's end, he had received the vote of every delegate – every delegate except himself! Exclaimed Mark Hanna: "Doesn't any of you realize that there's only one life between that madman and the Presidency!"[67]

★ ★ ★

157. **b. American imperialism.** The Democratic platform criticized the McKinley administration for promoting American imperialism around the world instead of supporting self-rule in other lands, particularly in lands acquired at the end of the Spanish-American War: Cuba and the Philippines. It demanded immediate independence for Cuba, and eventual independence for the Philippines.[68]

★ ★ ★

158. **b. renewed prosperity at home.** "Four More Years of the Full Dinner Pail!" was the Republican cry. McKinley and Roosevelt were voted in, 292 to 155 electoral votes. Theodore Roosevelt matched Bryan's energy, traveling 21,000 miles on the campaign trail, and electrifying crowds with his dynamic speaking style. Said one listener: " 'Has he been drinking?' 'Oh, no' was the answer, 'he needs no whiskey to make him feel that way – he intoxicates himself by his own enthusiasm.' "[69]

A Democrat was heard to say "that Mrs. Bryan would be sleeping in the White House after March 4th. 'If so,' cried a Republican in the crowd, 'she'll be sleeping with McKinley!' "[70]

1904

159. Theodore Roosevelt became President upon the assassination of William McKinley in 1901, the third Presidential assassination in 36 years. At the Republican convention of 1904 in Chicago he was nominated for President unanimously. His Democratic opponent was the Chief Justice of the New York Court of Appeals, Alton B. Parker. An important issue at the time, which both candidates favored, involved the building of the:

    a. Empire State Building.   **b.** Baltimore & Ohio Railroad.
    c. Panama Canal.   **d.** Erie Canal.

★ ★ ★

160. Theodore Roosevelt's election in 1904 was the most decisive victory since Andrew Jackson's defeat of Henry Clay in 1832. What was a major factor in Roosevelt's win?

    a. His energetic personality and great personal appeal
    b. An extended whistle stop campaign
    c. Endorsements by famous people
    d. A front porch campaign

★ ★ ★

161. Roosevelt had wide support around the country. Making broad use of executive powers, he had used the "bully pulpit" of the Presidency to act as no other President had before him. He enjoyed great popularity with the voters for his many accomplishments, including saving millions of acres of land for national parks, advocating reform in working conditions, mediating the coal workers' strike, and for:

    a. establishing the National Endowment for the Arts.
    b. breaking up the giant trusts.
    c. building the interstate highway system.
    d. promoting baseball as our national pastime.

159. **c. Panama Canal.** Negotiations to purchase a canal zone in Panama (then controlled by Columbia) had come to a standstill. However, Panama staged a revolt and, with aid from the United States, won its independence. In 1904 a treaty was signed with Panama for the purchase of land and the construction of a canal for $10 million, plus an increasing annual amount. The eradication of yellow fever and 90% of malaria in the area made the construction of the canal possible. At a cost of approximately $387 million - with 43,000 workers – the Panama Canal was completed in 1914, and was opened to traffic in 1920. In 1977 the Senate ratified a treaty returning the Canal Zone to Panama.[71] It was returned in 1999. ★ ★ ★

160. **a. His energetic personality and great personal appeal.** Roosevelt was immensely popular with the people. However, he feared he wouldn't receive the nomination in 1904, as he believed he had alienated some of the conservative Republican establishment. But the Republicans wanted to stick with a popular President. He himself was surprised by the magnitude of his win in 1904, and told his son Kermit, "I am stunned by the overwhelming victory we have won."[72] He maintained his boyish exuberance into adulthood, and once received this birthday greeting while he was President: "I congratulate you on attaining the respectable age of 46. You have made a very good start in life and your friends have great hopes for you when you grow up."[73] The electoral results in 1904 were 336 to 140; the popular vote was 56% to 38%. His opponent ran a lack-luster campaign, and Roosevelt received the greatest landslide since the counting of the popular vote began in 1824.
★ ★ ★

161. **b. breaking up the giant trusts.** Roosevelt was the first President to take action to regulate industry. In 1902, under the Sherman Anti-Trust Act of 1890, Roosevelt ordered a suit to dissolve the giant railroad monopoly Northern Securities Company. He wasn't anti-business, but wanted businesses to be regulated. As President, he filed a total of 45 anti-trust suits.

1908

<u>162.</u> William Jennings Bryan made his third run for the Presidency. At the Democratic convention, his supporters staged an 87-minute demonstration for him. Alas, he lost again! Bryan eventually became active as a defender of religious fundamentalism. At what famous event did he later appear?

　　a. The first radio broadcast in America
　　b. The first National Prayer Breakfast
　　c. The Scopes Trial
　　d. The National Debate Competition

★　　★　　★

<u>163.</u> Republican William Howard Taft of Ohio, Secretary of War in the Roosevelt administration, was Theodore Roosevelt's hand-picked successor. Taft's wife encouraged him to run for President. He reluctantly agreed, but the job he really wanted was:

　　a. Attorney General.　　b. Ambassador to Great Britain.
　　c. Secretary of State.　　d. a seat on the Supreme Court.

★　　★　　★

<u>164.</u> The campaign was not an exciting one, and centered mainly around the issue of:

　　a. who would carry on Theodore Roosevelt's policies.
　　b. who would stand up for American interests abroad.
　　c. the tariff.
　　d. the economy.

1908

162. **c. The Scopes Trial.** In 1925, Bryan appeared as special prosecutor opposite celebrated defense attorney Clarence Darrow, who defended schoolteacher John Scopes in the famous trial in Dayton, Tennessee. Scopes had agreed to be the defendant in a "test case" challenging a Tennessee law which prohibited the teaching of the theory of evolution. He was accused and convicted of teaching that theory, and was fined $100. Bryan did not compare well with Clarence Darrow at the trial, especially when he appeared as a witness to defend his belief in divine creation. Six days after the trial, Bryan died in his sleep. The verdict of "guilty" was overturned a year later by the Tennessee Supreme Court on a technicality, not on Constitutional grounds as Clarence Darrow had hoped. The Court found that the fine should have been determined by the jury, not the presiding judge. The case was then dismissed.[74]

★ ★ ★

163. **d. a seat on the Supreme Court.** Taking the advice of his wife, Taft agreed to be the Republican Presidential candidate. Mrs. Taft felt that if her husband served his party as President he would stand a better chance to be appointed to the Supreme Court. She was right. In June, 1921, Taft was appointed Chief Justice of the Supreme Court by President Warren G. Harding. He served from 1921 to 1930.

★ ★ ★

164. **a. who would carry on Theodore Roosevelt's policies.** Bryan claimed that many of Roosevelt's ideas were taken from the Democratic platform, and that he, Bryan, was the best person to continue those policies. Taft also promised to carry on with the Roosevelt programs and principles, but at a slower pace, and asserted that the American people could use a rest from the energetic Roosevelt years! Taft and his Vice-Presidential candidate, Representative James S. Sherman of New York, won the election, 321 to 162 electoral votes. Socialist Eugene Victor Debs received 420,000 votes – 3% of the vote.

1912

165. Disappointed in William Howard Taft's dismantling of his progressive policies, Theodore Roosevelt attempted to win the Republican nomination in 1912. However, the party leaders chose Taft, whereupon Roosevelt and other Republican progressives walked out of the convention, formed their own party and held their own convention. With Roosevelt as their candidate, the Progressive Party was also known as:

a. The Square Deal Party.   **b.** The Rough Rider Party.
c. The Big Moose Party.   **d.** The Bull Moose Party.

★   ★   ★

166. Woodrow Wilson, Governor of New Jersey and former President of Princeton University, was the Democratic nominee in 1912. He became only the second Democrat to be elected since the Civil War. What was a major factor in his win?

a. His reputation as Governor of New Jersey
b. His reputation as President of Princeton University
c. A split in the Republican vote between Taft and Roosevelt
d. Many Republicans voted for him.

★   ★   ★

167. With Eugene Victor Debs running again as the candidate of the Socialist Party, there were four major candidates. Which candidate was shot on his way to deliver a speech?

a. William Howard Taft   **b.** Theodore Roosevelt
c. Woodrow Wilson   **d.** Eugene Victor Debs

165. **d. The Bull Moose Party.** Upset with Taft and the Republicans for not following many of his progressive ideals, Roosevelt proclaimed: "My hat is in the ring!" He won 9 of 12 Republican primaries, but lost the nomination to Taft due to party politics. Declaring "I'm as fit as a bull moose!" Roosevelt, along with his supporters, bolted the Republican convention to run as a Progressive. Their platform included "primaries for all state and national offices; ... women's suffrage, limits on individual campaign contributions and campaign financial disclosure laws; ... opening congressional committee hearings to the public and recording committee votes; permitting Supreme Court decisions to be reversed by national referendum ... prohibition of child labor; a minimum wage for women; a six-day workweek and an eight-hour day;...a social security system;...(and) creation of a national health service;..."[75] This was the first convention in which women played a prominent role. ★ ★ ★

166. **c. A split in the Republican vote between Taft and Roosevelt.** The two Republicans together won the popular vote, but it was widespread. Wilson received 435 electoral votes, Roosevelt, 88, and Taft, 8. ★ ★ ★

167. **b. Theodore Roosevelt.** En route to a speech in Milwaukee, Roosevelt was shot in the chest. However, he insisted on proceeding to the auditorium to speak. A collective gasp filled the hall at the sight of his blood-stained shirt. "It takes more than that to kill a Bull Moose"[76] exclaimed TR. After speaking for an hour and a half, he was taken to a hospital. Roosevelt had spent years building himself up to combat childhood asthma; one of the doctors remarked: "It is largely due to the fact that he is a physical marvel that he was not dangerously wounded."[77] The bullet, deflected by the rolled up papers of his speech and an eyeglass case in his pocket, had lodged in a chest muscle. It was never removed. The would-be assassin, John N. Schrank, claimed that the ghost of McKinley had told him to avenge his assassination by killing his successor.[78]

1916

168. World War I had broken out in Europe. President Wilson was challenged by Supreme Court Justice Charles Evans Hughes, former Republican governor of New York. Woodrow Wilson ran on a slogan of:

a. "At peace in a world at war"   b. "Peace and prosperity"
c. "He kept us out of war."   d. "Stay out of war."

★   ★   ★

169. Charles Evans Hughes campaigned with the help of several new forms of media, including billboards, magazine ads and:

a. radio broadcasts.   b. brochures.
c. bumper stickers.   d. newsreels.

★   ★   ★

170. The Democratic platform included plans for a world association to promote international peace, which came to be known as:

a. The League of Nations.   b. The United Nations.
c. The Association of Nations.   d. The League of Peace

168. **c. "He kept us out of war."** With the outbreak of the First World War in Europe in 1914, Wilson and the country favored neutrality and hoped to stay out of the conflict. The Republicans claimed Wilson "kept us out of suffrage"[79] for his refusal to endorse the proposed Nineteenth Amendment to grant women the right to vote. Wilson wanted to leave the matter to the individual states. He once asked a member of his cabinet why he supported women's suffrage so strongly. His reply was: "I have two reasons...my mother and my wife!"[80]

★   ★   ★

169. d. newsreels. Having left his position on the United States Supreme Court to run for President, Hughes was later appointed Chief Justice by President Herbert Hoover, and served in that capacity from 1930 to 1941. Hughes was the only Justice to leave the Court and rejoin it at a later date.

The race in 1916 was close; Wilson prevailed, 277 to 254 electoral votes.   ★   ★   ★

170. **a. The League of Nations.** After the end of the First World War, Wilson promoted United States participation in the League during an exhaustive speaking tour in September, 1919. His health didn't hold up under the strain of the trip, and he was forced to return to Washington, where he suffered a series of three strokes. Incapacitated, he communicated his wishes on matters of importance through his wife for the remainder of his term. After the war ended in 1918, there was a debate in the Senate regarding ratification of both the Treaty of Versailles and the League of Nations. Wilson encountered resistance from Senators who feared "entangling alliances" with European powers by joining the League. Senator Henry Cabot Lodge of Massachusetts led the fight against the League, fearing that if we joined the League of Nations, American armed forces could be engaged without the consent of Congress.[81] Although Wilson fought hard for U. S. approval of the League, the Senate didn't ratify the peace treaty and the U. S. never joined the League.

1920

171. Republican Senator Warren G. Harding of Ohio and Governor Calvin Coolidge of Massachusetts faced Democratic Governor James M. Cox, also of Ohio. Who was Cox's soon to be well-known running mate?

> **a.** John W. Davis   **b.** Al Smith
> **c.** Harry Truman   **d.** Franklin D. Roosevelt

★   ★   ★

172. Harding, a former newspaper editor, was chosen at a deadlocked Republican convention - the remotest of "dark horse" candidates. Party leaders met on the thirteenth floor of the Blackstone Hotel in Chicago in a "smoke-filled room" and agreed on Harding. Who was instrumental in promoting his candidacy?

> **a.** Grass roots Republicans   **b.** Harding's wife
> **c.** Calvin Coolidge   **d.** William Howard Taft

★   ★   ★

173. What was different about voting in the election of 1920?

> **a.** The minimum voting age was changed.
> **b.** The polls closed early.
> **c.** Women could vote in national elections.
> **d.** No primaries were held.

171. **d. Franklin D. Roosevelt.** Assistant Secretary of the Navy during the Wilson administration, Roosevelt ran for Vice-President with Cox. The following year, Roosevelt contracted polio. After years of therapy and exercise, he made a political comeback and, in 1929, was elected Governor of New York and went on to win the Presidency in 1932. He never regained the use of his legs. ★ ★ ★

172. **b. Harding's wife.** Florence Kling Harding, along with campaign manager Harry Daugherty, persuaded Harding to enter the race. He wasn't certain he was up to the job, and didn't want the nomination, but went along with them. Everything went according to Daugherty's plan, as he worked endlessly to promote Harding at a deadlocked convention. He was nominated because . . . "he had no political enemies, he was popular, he represented a state crucial to Republicans, he had voted 'right,' that is, *for* Prohibition and women's suffrage."[82] Harding and Coolidge defeated Roosevelt and Cox, 404 to 127 electoral votes, but Harding's administration was rocked with scandal. In the famous Teapot Dome Scandal, his Secretary of the Interior sold federal oil reserves at Wyoming's Teapot Dome for personal gain. Harding was never found to have profited from the scandals. ★ ★ ★

173. **c. Women could vote in national elections.** Starting with Wyoming in 1869, women had been allowed to vote in some states. The Nineteenth Amendment assured women the right to vote in national elections in all states. Organized efforts for women's suffrage had begun in 1848 when Elizabeth Cady Stanton and Lucretia Mott called the Seneca Falls Convention in New York State. It called for women "to secure to themselves their sacred right to the elective franchise." After more than 70 years, their efforts – plus the efforts of Lucy Stone, *Battle Hymn of the Republic* author Julia Ward Howe, Susan B. Anthony, Carrie Chapman Catt and many others (including several men!) – finally won the right for all women to vote.[83] The Nineteenth Amendment went into effect in August, 1920.

1924

174. Meeting in New York in 1924, the Democrats set a convention record for:

    a. the most Vice-Presidential candidates ever.
    b. the most speeches ever.
    c. the shortest platform ever.
    d. the most ballots ever needed to nominate a major
       candidate.

★   ★   ★

175. Vice-President Calvin Coolidge had become President upon the death of Warren Harding in August, 1923. In July, 1924, the Republicans nominated Coolidge on the first ballot. "Keep Cool With Coolidge!" was their slogan. Their convention was:

    a. the only convention to be held in Washington, D.C.
    b. the first convention to be broadcast on radio.
    c. the first convention to be held in California.
    d. the first convention to be televised.

★   ★   ★

176. Former Ambassador to Great Britain John W. Davis, Democrat of West Virginia, challenged Calvin Coolidge. What helped Coolidge defeat Davis in 1924?

    a. Radio addresses
    b. An extensive speaking tour
    c. The prosperity of the Roaring Twenties
    d. A front porch campaign

174. **d. the most ballots ever needed to nominate a major candidate.** It also had the most speeches, demonstrations, fist-fights, committee meetings, hot dogs and soda pop in history![84] Forces of Governor Alfred E. Smith of New York (nominated in an electrifying speech by Franklin D. Roosevelt) and former Treasury Secretary William G. McAdoo of California battled each other. Neither candidate could reach the two-third's votes necessary for nomination. Deadlocked on the 100th ballot, both candidates withdrew, and the delegates settled on compromise candidate John W. Davis – on the 103rd ballot.

★ ★ ★

175. **b. the first convention to be broadcast on radio.** Meeting in Cleveland, the Republicans were the first to broadcast a political convention live on radio. Progressives came together from both parties and held their own convention, also in Cleveland; with 1,200 delegates and 9,000 spectators, they nominated Senator Robert M. LaFollette of Wisconsin for President. Their platform included the use of federal power to bring an end to private monopoly, an increase in the inheritance tax, equal rights for women, and international agreements to outlaw war, abolish conscription, and to disarm.[85] Considered a strong candidate, LaFollette received almost 5 million votes, one-sixth of the total popular vote, but won only the electoral votes of his home state, Wisconsin.

★ ★ ★

176. **c. The prosperity of the Roaring Twenties.** Times were so good that Coolidge didn't have to campaign. He defeated John W. Davis, 382 to 136 electoral votes, with 13 for LaFollette.

In 1924, all Native Americans born in the United States were granted citizenship, but some states claimed that those living on reservations were not state residents and could not vote. Some states denied them the right to vote because they were exempt from paying state taxes. It wouldn't be until the mid-1950's that every state gave Native Americans the right to vote.[86]

1928

177. Governor Alfred E. Smith, Democrat of New York, faced Secretary of Commerce, Republican Herbert Hoover of California. For what work was Hoover well-known during and after World War I?

    a. Manufacturing supplies for the U.S. Army
    b. Social work in New York City
    c. News reporting from the front
    d. Distribution of food and supplies to Europe

★ ★ ★

178. Hoover campaigned on the prosperity of the Republican administrations of Harding and Coolidge. What brought a major change in prosperity in 1929?

    a. The Panic of 1929
    b. The Floods of 1929
    c. The Stock Market Crash of 1929
    d. The Drought of 1929

★ ★ ★

179. An issue that dominated the election of 1928 was:

    a. Prohibition.   **b.** health care.
    c. taxes.   **d.** education.

1928

177. **d. Distribution of food and supplies to Europe.** As head of the American Relief Committee, Hoover provided assistance for approximately 120,000 Americans in Europe when World War I broke out. He distributed 34 million tons of American food, clothing and supplies as head of the Commission for the Relief of Belgium and as director of the American Relief Administration.[87]

Hoover won the electoral vote easily, 444 to 87.

★ ★ ★

178. **c. The stock market crash of 1929.** "A chicken in every pot and a car in every garage" promised the Republicans. Proclaimed Hoover: "We in America today are nearer to the final triumph over poverty than ever before in the history of any land...We shall soon...be in sight of the day when poverty will be banished from this nation."[88]

The stock market crashed on October 29, 1929, precipitating the worst depression in the history of the United States.

★ ★ ★

179. **a. Prohibition.** The Eighteenth Amendment, which took effect in January, 1920, signaled an end to the legal sale, transportation and commercial manufacture of liquor. Temperance societies in the United States had existed since before the Civil War. In 1851, the state of Maine passed a law prohibiting the sale of liquor, and twelve other states followed. A constitutional ban was advocated by the Prohibition Party, founded in 1869. The Anti-Saloon League of America pressured state legislatures to prohibit sales in the 1890's. Prohibition brought with it bootleg production, crime syndicates and corruption in government, and was virtually impossible to enforce.[89] Carry Nation was a well-known advocate of Prohibition. A large, imposing woman, she gained fame and notoriety in the early 1900's for attacking saloons with bricks, stones and hatchets! In 1928, Prohibition was opposed by Al Smith and supported by Herbert Hoover.

1932

180. Incumbent Republican Herbert Hoover was challenged by Democrat Franklin D. Roosevelt, Governor of New York. Energetic and confident, Roosevelt presented a vivid contrast to Hoover, who did too little too late to improve the nation's economy. What event of July, 1932 further hindered Hoover's chances of reelection?

    a. Another stock market crash
    b. The Bonus Marchers came to Washington.
    c. A tax increase
    d. Democrats singing "Happy Days Are Here Again"

★　★　★

181. How did Franklin Roosevelt break with tradition upon receiving the Democratic nomination for President?

    a. He asked his wife to give his acceptance speech.
    b. He didn't give an acceptance speech.
    c. He flew immediately to the convention in Chicago to accept the nomination.
    d. He waited a month to accept the nomination.

★　★　★

182. The Depression was THE issue in 1932. At its worst, what was the percentage of unemployed workers during the Depression?

    a. 10%   **b.** 15%   **c.** 20%   **d.** 25%

1932

180. b. The Bonus Marchers came to Washington. A group of approximately 15,000 World War I veterans came to Washington, D.C. to lobby for early payment of insurance bonuses promised them by Congress in 1924 (passed over the veto of Calvin Coolidge). They pitched camp near the Capitol, many with their families. However, Congress denied them the early payment. While some marchers left, many stayed on, whereupon President Hoover ordered the Army to disperse them. Makeshift shacks were set on fire, and one infant died from tear gas inhalation. Hoover was viewed as being insensitive to victims of the Depression for using armed force,[90] and his popularity declined even further.

★   ★   ★

181. c. He flew immediately to the convention in Chicago to accept the nomination. To show the delegates that he was a man of action, Roosevelt flew to Chicago and told them that he wanted to break the tradition of waiting several weeks to be formally notified of his nomination. "You have nominated me and I know it, and I am here to thank you for the honor. Let it also be symbolic that in so doing I broke tradition. Let it be from now on the task of our Party to break foolish traditions."[91] Speaker of the House John Nance Garner of Texas was nominated for Vice-President. On election day, Roosevelt and Garner swept the nation, 472 to 59 electoral votes, with a popular vote margin of 57% to 40%. The inauguration of 1933 was the last one to be held on March 4th.

★   ★   ★

182. d. 25%. In 1933, one quarter of the work force was unemployed. Businesses were forced to lay off workers due to decreased demand for their products, and many Americans were ruined financially.

1936

183. In an effort to bring the country out of the Great Depression, Franklin Roosevelt's administration created many government agencies that hired unemployed American workers. This program, which became a major issue of the election, was called:

    a. The New Deal.   **b.** The Fair Deal.

    b. The Roosevelt Deal.   **d.** Social Security.

★ ★ ★

184. Nominated for a second term, Franklin Roosevelt faced Republican Alf Landon, Governor of Kansas. Roosevelt's sweeping measures designed to get the country back on its feet were the main issues of the campaign. Unprecedented concessions to labor had become law, including the right to collective bargaining for trade unions, and a minimum wage that was established at:

    a. $ .30/hr. **b.** $ .50/hr. **c.** $1.00/hr. **d.** $2.00/hr.

★ ★ ★

185. Landon charged that Roosevelt was:

    a. too liberal.

    b. going to destroy the American system of government.

    c. spending too much money.

    d. too conservative.

183. **a. The New Deal.** In order to alleviate the social and financial crises of the Depression, the Roosevelt administration pushed numerous programs through Congress, among them the **Civilian Conservation Corps,** creating forestry projects for ¼ million unemployed, the **National Recovery Administration,** designed to set prices, wages, working hours and quality standards, and the **Tennessee Valley Authority,** which built dams and power stations to supply electricity to rural areas of the South.[92] In addition, the **Federal Communications Commission (FCC),** the **Federal Deposit Insurance Corporation (FDIC)** the **National Labor Relations Board (NLRB)** the **Securities and Exchange Commission (SEC)** and the **Social Security System** were created. Never before had the government taken such an active part in solving the nation's problems. Eventually, some of the New Deal programs were challenged, and were judged by the Supreme Court to be unconstitutional. Although the New Deal did not completely restore economic prosperity, it did avoid total economic collapse, and some of its programs remain with us today. The economy did not fully recover until the increase in federal defense spending for World War II.★ ★ ★

184. **a. $ .30/hr.**

★ ★ ★

185. **b. going to destroy the American system of government.** Landon disagreed with the methods of the New Deal, but agreed with its objectives. At their convention, the Democrats repealed the two-third's rule, which had plagued many front runners during the 19th century, and substituted a simple majority for nomination. After the re-nomination speech for FDR, there were fifty-six seconding speeches.[93] Roosevelt's charming and outgoing nature, along with his radio fireside chats, made him very popular with the voters. Landon carried Maine and Vermont. Roosevelt won an overwhelming victory – 523 to 8 electoral votes – carrying 60% of the popular vote. He took the oath of office in 1937 on the new inauguration date, January 20th.

1940

186. The Republican nominee in 1940 was Wendell Willkie of New York. The election centered around President Roosevelt's decision to:

    a. change his Vice-President. **b.** lend ships to England.
    c. close the banks.   **d.** run for a third term.

★　★　★

187. Franklin Roosevelt's popularity declined somewhat during his second term, in part due to his plan to:

    a. "pack" the Supreme Court.
    b. appoint conservatives to the Supreme Court.
    c. reorganize his Cabinet.
    d. redecorate the White House.

★　★　★

188. In international affairs, what issue played an important part in the campaign of 1940?

    a. Trade agreements   **b.** Relations with England
    c. The war in Europe   **d.** Relations with Latin America

1940

186. **d. run for a third term.** Willkie attacked Roosevelt for ignoring George Washington's two-term precedent. The Republican platform included attacks on the New Deal, on military unpreparedness of the Roosevelt administration, and called for constitutional amendments: one for equal rights for women, another to limit the president to two terms.[94] Willkie, a former Democrat who switched parties because he believed the Tennessee Valley Authority competed unfairly with the utility company of which he was president, had little political experience. "Better a third-termer than a third rater!" cried the Democrats. Willkie carried ten states; Roosevelt won again easily, 449 to 82 electoral votes, this time choosing Agriculture Secretary Henry Wallace of Iowa as his Vice-President.

★   ★   ★

187. **a. "pack" the Supreme Court.** Several New Deal agencies had been ruled unconstitutional by the Court; Roosevelt and members of his administration felt this was a deliberate challenge to the policies of the New Deal. He sent a plan to Congress whereby he could add up to six new judges – sympathetic to his views – up to a total of fifteen. Roosevelt was denounced for his "court-packing" scheme. Upon the retirement of a conservative justice, he dropped the idea, and, with the subsequent death and retirement of others on the Court, was able to make several appointments to the nine-member Court anyway.

★   ★   ★

188. **c. The war in Europe.** Germany had invaded Poland in September, 1939. In 1940, the Democratic platform called for the United States to stay out of the war in Europe, but to keep our defenses strong. Declared Roosevelt: "Your boys are not going to be sent to foreign wars."[95] Willkie claimed that Roosevelt had been weak on building the nation's defenses, but this strategy backfired when the Democrats reminded voters that many Republicans in Congress had voted against the administration's defense bills in the late 1930's.[96]

1944

189. Attacked by the Japanese at Pearl Harbor, Hawaii on December 7, 1941, the United States found itself at war. The Republicans turned to Governor Thomas E. Dewey of New York. Franklin Roosevelt was nominated by the Democrats for a fourth term, this time with Missouri Senator Harry Truman as his Vice-Presidential running mate. The Democrats emphasized Dewey's lack of experience in dealing with foreign affairs, and cried:

      a. "One more term!"
      b. "Roosevelt and experience!"
      c. "Don't change horses in mid-stream!"
      d. "Better stick with Roosevelt!"

★ ★ ★

190. Dewey and the Republicans accused Roosevelt of "incompetence, arrogance, inefficiency, fatigue, and senility" and Communist influence in his administration.[97] But Roosevelt – ever the master politician – turned the tables on his opponents and ridiculed them for accusing him of spending millions:

      a. on wasteful projects.
      b. on trips to meet other world leaders.
      c. on social security.
      d. to send a destroyer to pick up his dog.

★ ★ ★

191. Republicans also attacked Roosevelt on the grounds that:

      a. his administration was too secretive.
      b. he didn't understand the people.
      c. his health was failing.
      d. he lacked integrity.

1944

189. **c. "Don't change horses in mid-stream!"** The voters chose Roosevelt for a fourth term, continuing the trend that no President has lost a bid for reelection during time of war. The United States and its allies went on to win World War II in 1945.

It was estimated that over 2.5 million American soldiers voted from overseas by absentee ballot in 1944.[98]

★ ★ ★

190. **d. to send a destroyer to pick up his dog.** The Republicans charged that taxpayer money had been wasted when Roosevelt, after inspecting an Army-Navy joint command post off the Alaskan coast, had sent a destroyer to pick up his Scottish Terrier, Fala, supposedly left behind on an Aleutian Island. "These Republican leaders have not been content with attacks on me, or my wife, or on my sons. No...they now include my little dog, Fala. Well, of course, I don't resent attacks, but Fala does resent them. You know – you know – Fala's Scotch, and being a Scottie, as soon as he learned that the Republican fiction writers...had concocted a story that I had left him behind on an Aleutian Island and had sent a destroyer back to find him – at a cost to the taxpayers of two, or three, or eight or twenty million dollars – his Scotch soul was furious! He has not been the same dog since!"[99]

The war raged on, but the country smiled with FDR about his dog and about the Republicans, and returned him to the White House in November.

★ ★ ★

191. **c. his health was failing.** Twelve years in office had taken their toll. Roosevelt won, 432 to 99 electoral votes, but within three months of his inauguration he was dead of a cerebral hemorrhage.

1948

192. Vice-President Harry Truman assumed the Presidency upon the death of Franklin Roosevelt on April 12, 1945. World War II ended, the United Nations was founded and the Cold War, an economic and ideological struggle between East and West, had begun. Thomas Dewey ran for the Republicans again, this time against Harry Truman. Dewey was favored in the polls, and on election eve everyone thought he would win – everyone except:

    a. his best friend.   **b.** his wife.
    c. his campaign manager.   **d.** Harry Truman.

★ ★ ★

193. The Democratic platform called for civil rights for racial and religious minorities, with full protection of the law. Which delegate – a future Presidential candidate – led the fight on this issue?

    a. Hubert Humphrey   **b.** Lyndon Johnson
    c. Adlai Stevenson   **d.** Dwight D. Eisenhower

★ ★ ★

194. This newspaper's early edition headlines were "DEWEY DEFEATS TRUMAN":

    a. The New York Times   **b.** The Washington Post
    c. The Chicago Tribune   **d.** The Cleveland Plain Dealer

1948

192. d. Harry Truman.

★ ★ ★

193. a. **Hubert Humphrey.** Minneapolis mayor Hubert Humphrey led the fight for the inclusion of a civil rights plank in the Democratic platform. Thirty-five southerners from Mississippi and Alabama walked out in protest. Strom Thurmond, Democratic Governor and later Senator from South Carolina, was among those that walked out. In 1948 he ran for President for the States' Rights, or Dixiecrat Party. Former Vice-President Henry Wallace also ran - as a Progressive. The Republicans agreed with Democrats on some issues, including a call for arms control, and recognition of the new state of Israel.

Truman received 303 electoral votes to 189 for Dewey, with 39 going to Strom Thurmond. Wallace won 2% of the popular vote.

★ ★ ★

194. c. **The Chicago Tribune.** Confident in its prediction that Dewey had won, the Chicago Tribune printed its early edition with the headline: "Dewey Defeats Truman."

When the paper was printed, it wasn't known that California and Ohio had voted for Truman, giving him the victory. Complaining about the "Do-Nothing Congress," Truman traveled the country in an extended whistle stop campaign. His victory was the greatest upset in Presidential history. As shown in a famous photo, it was a smiling Harry Truman that held up a copy of the Chicago Tribune for all to see!

1952

195. Harry Truman chose not to run again, and the Democrats nominated Governor Adlai Stevenson of Illinois, (grandson of Grover Cleveland's Vice-President, Adlai Stevenson). His opponent, Republican Dwight D. Eisenhower, had never held public office, but was well-known during World War II for serving as:

    a. advisor to the President.   **b.** Supreme Allied Commander.
    c. Secretary of Defense.   **d.** Army Chief of Staff.

★ ★ ★

196. During the campaign, Eisenhower's running mate, Senator Richard M. Nixon of California, was accused of keeping an $18,000 fund of private contributions that was used for personal expenses; it was thought that he might be dropped from the ticket. Appearing on national television, Nixon defended himself in a speech that came to be known as:

    a. the Nixon Speech.   **b.** the $18,000 Speech.
    c. the Secret Fund Speech.   **d.** the Checkers Speech.

★ ★ ★

197. The country had become involved in the Korean War. Peace negotiations were deadlocked. What did Eisenhower say he would do if elected?

        a. "I shall send a representative to Korea."
        b. "I shall end the Korean War."
        c. "I shall go to Korea."
        d. "I shall not negotiate with Korea."

1952

195. **b. Supreme Allied Commander.** Eisenhower was extremely popular as a general during World War II, and for mounting the D-Day invasion of the Normandy beaches in June, 1944 as Supreme Allied Commander. Both the Democratic and Republican parties were interested in him as a presidential candidate in 1948 and in 1952. After the war, Eisenhower served as President of Columbia University from 1948-50, and as Supreme Commander of the North Atlantic Treaty Organization (NATO) from 1951 until his nomination for President in 1952.

★ ★ ★

196. **d. The Checkers Speech.** In a television appearance in which he denied any misuse of the $18,000 fund, Nixon listed his personal assets and added that there was one gift he had received – a Cocker Spaniel that his six-year old daughter Tricia had named "Checkers" – that his family was not going to give back. After the speech, many viewers called the Republican National Committee with their support, and Eisenhower kept Nixon on the ticket.[100]

★ ★ ★

197. **c. "I shall go to Korea."** Eisenhower pledged to travel to Korea personally to restart the peace talks. He went there in December, 1952. An armistice was signed in July, 1953, in which North and South Korea were separated by a demilitarized zone at the 38th parallel, approximately the same boundary that existed before hostilities broke out.[101] The election of 1952 marked the first time that television was used to promote a candidate. Adlai Stevenson, brilliant and well-informed on the issues, did not play as well on TV as did Eisenhower's smile and folksy manner. "Let's talk sense to the American people," said Stevenson. "Let's tell them the truth, that there are no gains without pains, that this is the eve of great decisions, not easy decisions."[102] Eisenhower (nicknamed "Ike") prevailed at the polls, 442 to 89 electoral votes. "I Like Ike!" was the slogan of the Republicans.

1956

198. Once again the Democrats turned to Adlai Stevenson to challenge Dwight Eisenhower, now the incumbent. Stevenson threw the choice for Vice-President to the Democratic convention. A close contest followed between Tennessee Senator Estes Kefauver and which soon to be well-known Senator?

>   **a.** Robert F. Kennedy   **b.** Lyndon B. Johnson
>   **c.** John F. Kennedy   **d.** Hubert H. Humphrey

★   ★   ★

199. President Eisenhower had suffered a heart attack in September, 1955. In order to dispel rumors about his health, he traveled to thirteen states during the campaign. Adlai Stevenson called for a halt to atmospheric testing of nuclear weapons and for:

>   **a.** an all volunteer army.   **b.** a continuation of the draft
>   **c.** reduced taxes.   **d.** space exploration.

★   ★   ★

200. President Eisenhower campaigned on the successes and accomplishments of his administration, including peace and prosperity, the end of the Korean War, extending Social Security, a surplus in the budget of 1956, and:

>   **a.** statehood for Alaska and Hawaii.
>   **b.** federal funding for the arts.
>   **c.** development of the interstate highway system.
>   **d.** space travel.

1956

198. **c. John F. Kennedy.** After delivering the nominating speech for Adlai Stevenson, Senator John F. Kennedy of Massachusetts was a contender for the Vice-Presidential nomination. He came very close to winning, but eventually lost to Estes Kefauver.

★ ★ ★

199. a. an all volunteer army. At the 1956 Democratic convention Stevenson spoke about " 'a New America' where 'poverty is abolished,' 'freedom is made real for everybody,' and the ancient idea 'that men can solve their differences by killing each other' is discarded."[103] Eisenhower opposed Stevenson's proposal for an all volunteer army, and criticized his call for an end to atmospheric nuclear testing, although Eisenhower later requested a nuclear test ban.

★ ★ ★

200. c. development of the interstate highway system. During the first Eisenhower administration, thousands of miles of interstate highways were built, linking the country by automobile.

In 1954 the destructive McCarthy hearings - led by Wisconsin Republican Senator Joseph McCarthy - came to an end. His sensational "investigations" for alleged Communist influence in the government were finally brought to a halt when televised hearings exposed his bullying tactics and counsel for the Army Joseph Welch asked him: "Have you left no sense of decency?"[104]

Eisenhower won easily, 457 to 73 electoral votes.

1960

<u>201.</u>   John F. Kennedy won the Democratic presidential nomination and chose Texas Senator Lyndon Johnson as his running mate.   Their opponents were Republican Vice-President Richard Nixon of California and U.N. Ambassador Henry Cabot Lodge of Massachusetts.   What played a major role in the election?

      a. TV advertising   **b.** Bus campaigns
      c. Whistle-stop campaigns   **d.** Televised debates

★ ★ ★

<u>202.</u> What incident led to the support of Kennedy by African-Americans at the polls?

      a. The arrest of Martin Luther King, Jr.
      b. A march in Washington
      c. An endorsement speech by Martin Luther King, Jr.
      d. A campaign stop in Martin Luther King, Jr.'s home town

★ ★ ★

<u>203.</u>   Two of the main issues of the campaign were the Communist threat and the economy.   In addition, an issue was made of the fact that:

      a. Kennedy was wealthy.   **b.** Nixon was not wealthy.
      c. Kennedy was Catholic.   **d.** Nixon was a Quaker.

1960

201. **d. Televised debates.** The candidates agreed to a series of four televised debates, which were also aired on radio. Kennedy appeared self-confident and relaxed. Nixon, who had recently been hospitalized due to an infection from a leg injury, appeared haggard and tired. Over 100 million Americans heard the debates, the first ever Presidential debates shown on television. Many radio listeners felt that Nixon had won, while most television viewers believed Kennedy had won. Kennedy himself believed that if it had not been for the debates he would have lost. Kennedy, who had distinguished himself by saving the lives of several of his PT boat crew members in the Pacific during World War II, became the youngest person ever to be elected President. ★ ★ ★

202. **a. The arrest of Martin Luther King, Jr.** In October, he was arrested at a sit-in in a segregated restaurant in Atlanta. At the news of this, Kennedy called Mrs. King; Robert Kennedy, the candidate's brother, was able to arrange for King's release on bail. Upon hearing what the Kennedy's had done for his son, Martin Luther King, Sr. switched his support from Nixon to Kennedy, and African-Americans supported Kennedy in November.[105] ★ ★ ★

203. **c. Kennedy was Catholic.** However, Kennedy responded by declaring his belief in the separation of church and state. Some believed that Kennedy's wealthy father was contributing too much to his campaign effort; Kennedy told an audience that he had received a letter from his father saying: "Dear Jack: Don't buy a single vote more than is necessary. I'll be damned if I'm going to pay for a landslide."[106] At one stop, Kennedy was greeted by a group of enthusiastic children. He proclaimed: "If we can lower the voting age to nine, we are going to sweep this state."[107] Kennedy won by a razor thin popular vote margin, 49.7% to 49.5%, and by an electoral vote of 303 to 219. Independent candidate Senator Harry F. Byrd of Virginia received 15 electoral votes.

1964

204. The country was shocked and saddened by the assassination of President Kennedy in Dallas on November 22, 1963. Vice-President Lyndon Johnson became President, and received the Democratic nomination in 1964. His challenger, Republican Senator Barry Goldwater of Arizona, was considered to be:

a. a great speaker.   b. progressive.
c. very conservative.   d. very liberal.

★ ★ ★

205. What area of the United States voted for the first time in 1964?

a. Alaska   b. Hawaii
c. Puerto Rico   d. The District of Columbia

★ ★ ★

206. Barry Goldwater's proposals included voluntary Social Security, a more aggressive policy to drive the Communists out of South Vietnam, and a foreign policy that considered the possibilities of using:

a. conventional warfare.
b. international peace negotiations
c. international trade agreements.
d. nuclear weapons.

1964

204. **c. very conservative.** Republicans displayed photos of Goldwater with the words: "In your heart, you know he's right." The Democrats responded, "Yes – extreme right."[108] Even though Goldwater eventually attempted to reverse his stand on some issues, such as leaving the United Nations and breaking off relations with the Soviet Union, many voters had been alienated, and his popularity remained at a very low level.

★ ★ ★

205. **d. The District of Columbia.** The voters in the District of Columbia had never had the right to vote in Presidential elections. On March 29, 1961, the Twenty-third Amendment was ratified, giving the District the right to vote.

★ ★ ★

206. **d. nuclear weapons.** By this time the United States had a military presence in Vietnam. During the campaign, Barry Goldwater was very straightforward in his comments, and at one point said he wouldn't be afraid to "use 'low yield nuclear bombs' if necessary to fight the Communists in Vietnam and elsewhere'...."[109] Democratic TV commercials depicted Goldwater as someone who was ready to push "the button" and start a nuclear war. Republicans said: "In your heart, you know he's right." Democrats replied: "In your heart, you know he might."[110] In his acceptance speech, Goldwater declared: "...extremism in the defense of liberty is no vice!" - to which a reporter remarked: "My God! He's going to run as Barry Goldwater!"[111] Lyndon Johnson was viewed as a peace candidate compared to Goldwater. Along with Vice-Presidential candidate Senator Hubert Humphrey of Minnesota, Johnson won by a huge popular vote margin, winning 61% to Goldwater's 39%. The electoral vote was 486 to 52.

1968

207. After almost losing the New Hampshire primary to Minnesota Senator Eugene McCarthy, Lyndon Johnson decided against running for reelection. McCarthy won approximately half of the primaries. Who won the other half?

    a. Robert Kennedy   **b.** Hubert Humphrey
    c. George McGovern   **d.** Edmund Muskie

★   ★   ★

208. By 1968 the country was heavily involved in Vietnam, with ½ million American troops there. Delegates at the Democratic convention in Chicago were divided over the war, while outside the convention hall 5,000 anti-war protesters clashed with police. Richard Nixon was nominated again by the Republicans, with Maryland's Governor Spiro Agnew as his running-mate. Who was the Democratic presidential nominee in 1968?

    a. Edmund Muskie   **b.** George McGovern
    c. Hubert Humphrey   **d.** Eugene McCarthy

★   ★   ★

209. Which third party candidate received over 13% of the popular vote, and 46 electoral votes?

    a. Eugene McCarthy   **b.** Strom Thurmond
    c. Nelson Rockefeller   **d.** George Wallace

1968

207. **a. Robert Kennedy.** A peace candidate, the brother of President John F. Kennedy – and now Senator from New York - Robert Kennedy had entered the race. His campaign was going well when it all came to a sudden and tragic end when he was assassinated on June 6, 1968 following his victory in the California primary.

★ ★ ★

208. **c. Hubert Humphrey.** Mayor of Minneapolis, Senator from Minnesota, and Vice-President of the United States, Hubert Humphrey was a champion of civil rights legislation. Among his proposals in Congress were the concept of a Peace Corps (in the late 1950's) and medical insurance for seniors; he was a consistent supporter of arms control, humanitarian aid, welfare legislation and aid to small businesses. Early in the campaign, Richard Nixon was well ahead in the polls; Humphrey was associated with the Vietnam policies of the Johnson administration, which had become unpopular. It wasn't until he began to distance himself from Johnson's policies, and proposed that we halt the bombing of North Vietnam before seeing a show of good faith by the North, that he began to improve in the polls.

★ ★ ★

209. **d. George Wallace.** Governor of Alabama, Democrat George Wallace split with his party and ran as the candidate of the American Independent Party, advocating law and order, victory in Vietnam and opposing busing for the purpose of achieving racial segregation. As the election approached, Hubert Humphrey was closing the gap between himself and Nixon. On election day the popular vote was very close, but the electoral vote was 310 to 191 in favor of Nixon. Wallace did well for a third party candidate, winning 46 electoral votes.

1972

<u>210.</u> Senator George McGovern of South Dakota was chosen by the Democrats to challenge incumbent Richard Nixon. American forces were still fighting in Vietnam. What did McGovern promise to do about the war if elected?

    a. Continue Nixon's policies.
    b. Pull all American forces out of Vietnam immediately.
    c. Increase the number of U.S. troops there.
    d. Decrease the number of U.S. troops there.

★　★　★

<u>211.</u> The election of 1972 was the first election in which:

    a. opinion polls were conducted.
    b. eighteen year-olds had the right to vote.
    c. candidates were interviewed on television.
    d. candidates traveled the country by bus.

★　★　★

<u>212.</u> Richard Nixon was way ahead in the polls. However, on July 17, 1972, five men were arrested for breaking into the Democratic National Committee Offices at the Watergate Office Building in Washington, D.C. For what committee did these men work?

    a. The Committee to Reelect the President
    b. The Committee for National Security
    c. The Republican National Committee
    d. The Watergate Break-in Committee

210. b. **Pull all American forces out of Vietnam immediately.**
Richard Nixon had been decreasing the number of U.S. troops in
Vietnam since 1969. By the end of 1972, American troop levels
were down to 24,000. The Democratic platform "favored
amnesty for those who had refused to enter the service (once
American troops and prisoners of war were safely home) ...
busing to achieve racial integration in the public schools,
abolishing capital punishment, banning the sale of handguns,"
and stated "Americans should be free to make their own choices
of lifestyles...without being subject to discrimination or
prosecution."[112] McGovern's views were moderate compared to
many delegates who supported him at the convention, but the
Republicans were able to portray him as a radically leftist
candidate. The Republican platform favored "a volunteer army,
arms control, ... full employment while opposing busing to
achieve racial balance, national health insurance, and complete
withdrawal of U.S. forces from Vietnam without the return of
the prisoners of war."[113]   ★   ★   ★

211. b. **eighteen year-olds had the right to vote.** The Twenty-
sixth Amendment to the Constitution, ratified on June 30, 1971,
lowered the voting age from 21 to 18. Less than half of the 18 to
20 year-olds voted in 1972. ★   ★   ★

212. a. **The Committee to Reelect the President.** Richard Nixon
was on his way to a landslide, yet members of the Committee to
Reelect the President burglarized the Democratic National
Headquarters in July, 1972. Nevertheless, Nixon won with ease
in November, 520 to 17 electoral votes. Libertarian John Hospers
received one electoral vote. Other misconduct on behalf of the
President was eventually revealed: installing eavesdropping
devices at Democratic headquarters, giving cover-up money to
Watergate defendants, creating problems for well-known
political and entertainment personalities on an "enemies list,"
and burglarizing the office of psychiatrist Daniel Ellsberg, who
gave the Pentagon Papers (classified information regarding the
origins of the war in Vietnam) to the press.[114]

1976

213. On August 9, 1974, under the threat of impeachment hearings over the Watergate break-in scandal, Richard Nixon resigned the Presidency. Vice-President Gerald Ford received the Republican nomination for President in 1976. How had Ford become Vice-President?

>   **a.** There had been a recall election for Vice-President.
>   **b.** Spiro Agnew had retired while in office.
>   **c.** Richard Nixon had named Ford to replace Spiro Agnew, who had resigned in 1973.
>   **d.** Ford ran with Nixon in 1972.

★ ★ ★

214. At the Democratic convention, dark horse Jimmy Carter, former Governor of Georgia, received enough delegate support during the primaries to be nominated for President on the first ballot. His Vice-Presidential running mate was Minnesota Senator Walter Mondale. What did Jimmy Carter emphasize during the campaign that helped him win the election?

>   **a.** His life as a peanut farmer
>   **b.** His years as Governor of Georgia
>   **c.** The fact that he was a Washington "outsider"
>   **d.** The fact that he had a great smile

★ ★ ★

215. A turning point occurred in one of the Presidential debates when President Ford was asked a question about:

>   **a.** taxes.
>   **b.** Soviet domination of Eastern Europe.
>   **c.** defense spending.
>   **d.** education.

1976

213. c. Richard Nixon had named Ford to replace Spiro Agnew, who had resigned in 1973. Agnew had resigned amid allegations of corruption before and during his term as Governor of Maryland. In order to avoid criminal prosecution, Agnew resigned the Vice-Presidency and pleaded "no contest" to one count of tax evasion. Gerald Ford had served in the United States House of Representatives for 24 years before becoming Vice-President, including eight years as House Minority Leader, from 1965 to 1973.

★ ★ ★

214. c. the fact that he was a Washington "outsider." Carter hadn't spent time in Washington, and when the campaign started, he wasn't very well-known. When he first entered the race, people asked: "Jimmy who?" Carter said that when he told his own mother he was running for President, she answered: "President of what?"[115] But he turned the fact that he was not nationally well-known into an asset, and everywhere he went he became famous for saying: "My name is Jimmy Carter and I'm running for President." During the primaries he declared: "I'll never tell a lie," to which one of his supporters replied: "We're gonna lose the liar vote!"[116]

"A Leader for a Change" and "Not Just Peanuts!" were his slogans.

★ ★ ★

215. b. Soviet domination of Eastern Europe. During the second Presidential debate, at a time when several Eastern European countries were living under Soviet dominated communist rule, Ford stated that there was "no Soviet domination of Eastern Europe, . . . and there will never be under a Ford administration."[117] That statement followed Ford for the rest of the campaign. That, along with his pardon of Richard Nixon over the Watergate scandal, damaged his chances of election in 1976. Carter and Mondale won, 297 to 240 electoral votes. An undeclared candidate – Ronald Reagan - received one electoral vote.

1980

216. What Middle East crisis contributed to Jimmy Carter's defeat at the polls in November?

    a. The Iraq hostage crisis   **b.** The Iran hostage crisis
    c. The Iraq Contra Scandal   **d.** The Iran Contra Scandal

★ ★ ★

217. Which 10-term Republican Congressman ran for President as an Independent in 1980, selecting a Democrat as his running mate?

    a. Howard Baker   **b.** John Anderson
    c. John Connally   **d.** Bob Dole

★ ★ ★

218. Governor Ronald Reagan of California was the Republican nominee, along with his Vice-Presidential candidate, George H. W. Bush. Which voters helped Reagan and Bush gain a victory in 1980?

    a. Reagan Democrats   **b.** Bush Democrats
    c. Independents   **d.** Liberals

1980

216. **b. The Iran hostage crisis.** In addition, Jimmy Carter had inherited rising inflation and stagnant growth in the economy. He had cut spending and raised taxes, to no avail. Arab members of OPEC had banned oil exports to countries supporting Israel - which had been attacked in 1973 - causing long lines at the pumps in the U.S.

★   ★   ★

217. **b. John Anderson.** A moderate candidate, he favored liberal social and foreign policies, and conservative economic policies. At one point in the campaign, his ratings in several polls were over 20%. Although Anderson won close to 6 million votes, they were widespread and he received no electoral votes.

★   ★   ★

218. **a. Reagan Democrats.** Democrats who voted for Reagan, mostly in the South and West, helped him win. During the campaign Reagan repeatedly quoted Democrats Franklin D. Roosevelt and John F. Kennedy. The results of the popular vote were: Reagan, 51%, Carter, 41%, Anderson, 7%. The electoral vote was 489 for Reagan, 49 for Carter.

1984

219. Former Vice-President Walter Mondale of Minnesota received the Democratic nomination. What was unique about his choice for Vice-President?

    a. He chose a Republican.
    b. He chose a Libertarian.
    c. He chose an unknown candidate.
    d. He chose the first woman to run for national office.

★ ★ ★

220. Mondale attacked the Reagan administration for wasteful military buildup and for failing to reach an arms control agreement with the Soviet Union. In 1983, Reagan had proposed the Strategic Defense Initiative, which opponents referred to as:

    a. Star Wars.   **b.** Star Defense.
    c. Defense Wars.   **d.** Space Wars.

★ ★ ★

221. During the campaign, the Republicans and Democrats reversed their traditional roles regarding:

    a. taxes.   **b.** social programs.
    c. budget deficits.   **d.** health care.

1984

219. **d. He chose the first woman to run for national office.** Congresswoman Geraldine Ferraro of New York was the Democratic Vice-Presidential nominee in 1984.

★　★　★

220. **a. Star Wars.** The Strategic Defense Initiative was designed as a space-based nuclear defense system. Many viewed the proposal as an escalation of the arms race.

★　★　★

221. **c. budget deficits.** Traditionally, Republicans had assailed Democratic administrations for deficit spending, but Ronald Reagan, while calling for tax cuts and cuts in social programs, had amassed huge budget deficits due to increased military spending. For the most part, Reagan ignored the deficit during the campaign. Inflation was down and employment was up; Reagan had cut taxes for the wealthiest, however the average taxpayer had seen a rise in their tax rates.

Mondale's proposals included a raise in taxes on corporations and on upper income individuals in order to reduce the deficit, the largest in our history up to that time. Reagan pledged no tax raises, except as a last resort.[118]

The candidates also reversed the traditional roles of their parties regarding the tariff. For 100 years the Democrats had favored reduced trade barriers and the promotion of global free trade. In 1984 they called for protectionist measures, most of which were opposed by Reagan.[119]

With the hope of winning all 50 states, Reagan followed Harry Truman's whistle-stop campaign in Ohio, even using the same train in an apparent effort to win Democratic votes.[120] A former actor and movie star, he played well on television, and succeeded in projecting an image of confidence to the American people, and courage in standing up to the Soviet Union. He prevailed again at the polls, receiving 59% of the popular vote, and an electoral victory of 525 to 13.

1988

222. Republican Vice-President George H. W. Bush and Senator Dan Quayle of Indiana opposed Democratic Governor of Massachusetts Michael Dukakis and Senator Lloyd Bentsen of Texas. With a victory at the polls in November, George Bush became the:

    a. first Texan to become President.
    b. first sitting Vice-President to be elected since
        Martin van Buren in 1836.
    c. first World War II veteran to become President.
    d. first former U.S. representative to become President.

★ ★ ★

223. What pledge did George H. W. Bush make in the 1988 campaign?

    a. Read my mind – no new taxes!
    b. Read my lips – no new wars!
    c. Read my lips – no new taxes!
    d. Read my book – it's on sale!

★ ★ ★

224. George Bush started out stressing religion and patriotism, while Michael Dukakis detailed a health insurance plan, including employer-financed health insurance. Negative TV advertising by the Republicans attacked Dukakis regarding a controversial:

    a. prison furlough program in Massachusetts.
    b. education plan in Massachusetts.
    c. health care plan in Massachusetts.
    d. national defense plan.

1988

222. **b. first sitting Vice-President to be elected since Martin van Buren in 1836.** Among his other positions before becoming Vice-President were Ambassador to the United Nations and Director of the Central Intelligence Agency. As a member of the naval air service during World War II, Bush flew fifty-eight combat missions, including one mission where he bailed out over the South Pacific after his torpedo bomber was hit by enemy fire. He was rescued by a U.S. submarine.

★ ★ ★

223. **c. Read my lips – no new taxes!** However, President Bush eventually agreed, in June, 1990, to raise taxes on gasoline, cigarettes and beer; he raised Medicare premiums, added new luxury taxes and increased the highest income tax rates – in order to reduce the growing federal deficit. He subsequently referred to the decision to raise taxes as a mistake.[121]

★ ★ ★

224. **a. prison furlough program in Massachusetts.** The ad was very damaging to Dukakis and his campaign. George Bush won the election by an electoral vote of 426 to 111. Lloyd Bentsen received one electoral vote for President.

1992

225. Bill Clinton, Democratic Governor of Arkansas, and his running mate, Senator Al Gore of Tennessee, challenged incumbents George H. W. Bush and Dan Quayle. At the campaign's outset, George Bush enjoyed great popularity due to:

    a. 1,000 Points of Light.   **b.** the economy.
    c. the Gulf War.   **d.** education spending.

★ ★ ★

226. Bill Clinton turned out to be an enthusiastic campaigner as he presented his views for moving the country forward. The issue that most contributed to his win in November was:

    a. the economy.   **b.** defense spending.
    c. welfare reform.   **d.** college loans.

★ ★ ★

227. Texas businessman Ross Perot entered the race as an independent. This was the first time a third party candidate:

    a. spoke with a big accent.   **b.** made a serious challenge.
    c. received no electoral votes.   **d.** led in the polls.

1992

225. **c. the Gulf War.** In response to the Iraqi invasion of Kuwait on August 2, 1990, the United States joined with 27 other nations to send troops to Saudi Arabia in what was known as operation "Desert Shield." The United States contributed $7 billion to the war effort, while its allies spent $54 billion.[122] George Bush enjoyed his highest approval ratings after the Gulf War – 89%.

★　★　★

226. **a. the economy.** With high approval ratings, Bush delayed campaigning until early 1992; but by this time, the country had fallen into a recession. The deficit under Ronald Reagan had grown from $1 trillion to $4 trillion, and increasing estimates for bailing out hundreds of savings and loans that had become insolvent due to corruption, mismanagement, or competition – as a result of deregulation in the early 1980's – further reduced Bush's popularity. (The General Accounting Office cost estimate to bail out the savings and loans was $500 billion over 40 years).

★　★　★

227. **d. led in the polls.** Texas businessman Ross Perot staged a strong third party challenge. Decrying the government's massive deficit spending, Perot won 19% of the popular vote, the highest percentage of any third party candidate since Theodore Roosevelt's 27% in 1912. At the outset he led in the polls, but after dropping out of the race and re-entering later in the campaign, Perot never regained his lead. The election of 1992 marked the first time in decades that so many newspapers endorsed the Democratic candidate. Bill Clinton brought back Democrats who had voted for Reagan. With a platform that included deficit reduction through economic growth, universal access to health care, unpaid leave for family emergencies, aid to education, job training, a tax increase for the wealthiest 2% of Americans and modest tax cuts for the middle class, Clinton received 370 electoral votes to 168 for George Bush.

1996

228. Incumbent Bill Clinton was challenged by Republican Senator Bob Dole of Kansas and his running mate Jack Kemp, a former Congressman from New York and a former professional football player. During the campaign, Clinton defended his record on the economy, which included the creation of:

        a. 1 million new jobs.   **b.** 3 million new jobs.
        c. 5 million new jobs.   **d.** 10 million new jobs.

★   ★   ★

229. Republican challenger Bob Dole holds a record in the U.S. Senate for:

    a. the longest speech.
    b. the longest filibuster.
    c. the longest term as leader of the Republican Party.
    d. the longest term as chairman of a committee.

★   ★   ★

230. During his first administration, Bill Clinton signed into law a deficit reduction plan that:

    a. reduced the deficit by $100 billion.
    b. reduced the deficit by $300 billion.
    c. was the smallest deficit reduction plan ever.
    d. was the largest deficit reduction plan ever:
        over $600 billion.

1996

228. **d. 10 million new jobs.** Among the legislation signed into law during the first Clinton administration were: the Family and Medical Leave Act, providing over 42 million Americans with twelve weeks of unpaid leave for childbirth, adoption, or personal or family illness; the 1993 Economic Plan, which included a cut in taxes for 15 million working Americans; an Assault Weapons Ban; the Brady Bill, which imposed a five-day waiting period on handgun purchases for background checks; and the Direct Student Loan Program, under which low interest tuition loans can be repaid with future salary earnings. In addition, the federal bureaucracy was cut, and crime rates were lowered.

★ ★ ★

229. **c. the longest term as leader of the Republican Party.** First elected to Congress in 1961, he served in the House of Representatives until 1969, and in the United States Senate from 1969 to 1996. He was Republican leader in the Senate for twelve years, from 1984 to 1996.

A second lieutenant in the Army during World War II, Bob Dole received two Purple Hearts for injuries sustained, and the Bronze Star Medal for trying to help a fallen soldier in combat.

★ ★ ★

230. **d. was the largest deficit reduction plan ever: over $600 billion.** Bill Clinton was reelected, 379 to 159 electoral votes. Ross Perot, running as the candidate of the Reform Party, received 8 million popular votes and no electoral votes.

2000

231. Vice-President Al Gore received the Democratic nomination, and chose Senator Joseph Lieberman of Connecticut as his running mate. They were opposed by George W. Bush, Republican Governor of Texas (son of former President George H. W. Bush), and Vice-Presidential candidate Dick Cheney, former Representative from Wyoming. The election turned out to be one of the most controversial Presidential elections ever. The vote of which state was at the center of the controversy?

a. Texas **b.** New York **c.** California **d.** Florida

★   ★   ★

232. What body played a major role in deciding the outcome of the election of 2000?

a. The Supreme Court **b.** The House of Representatives
c. The Senate   **d.** The Congress, in joint session

★   ★   ★

233. During the vote count, a controversy developed regarding ballots that were difficult to read, mainly due to a problem with:

a. falling chads.   **b.** suspended chads.
c. hanging chads.   **d.** waving chads.

2000

231. d. Florida. There were many issues discussed in 2000, but the Florida vote count controversy was the most memorable event of the election. Among the campaign proposals made by Al Gore were: ensuring Medicare's solvency through 2030, using part of the budget surplus to fund prescription drug benefits for Medicare recipients, paying off the national debt by 2012, and opposing private retirement accounts for Social Security. George Bush's proposals included a choice between federal and private prescription drug benefit plans for Medicare recipients, semi-privatization of Social Security, a ten-year $1.3 trillion tax cut, and elimination of the national debt by 2016.[123]

★   ★   ★

232. a. The Supreme Court. Al Gore received approximately 540,000 more popular votes than George W. Bush, but the final electoral vote count was in question. It ultimately came down to the vote in Florida, where Bush's brother Jeb was governor. Bush had been given Florida's electoral votes, but disputed vote counts prompted recounts in several Florida counties. However, hand recounting of votes was challenged by the Bush campaign, and the issue of whether or not to recount made its way to the United States Supreme Court. At 10:00 p.m. on December 12th – two hours before the deadline for certifying Florida's electors – with George Bush ahead in Florida by 537 votes, the Supreme Court handed down a 5-4 decision to halt the hand recount of votes in Florida, thus giving the election – and the Presidency - to Bush. The final electoral vote was 271 for Bush, 266 for Gore. A vote was withheld by one elector - to protest the lack of voting representation in Congress for the District of Columbia.

★   ★   ★

233. c. hanging chads. Many punch card ballots had not been completely punched out. Hanging chads are punched out pieces still attached by one corner; swinging chads: two corners are attached; tri chads: three corners are attached; pregnant chads: the hole was punched through but the chad is attached at all four corners; dimpled chads: attached chads with a dimple!

2004

234. Republican incumbent George W. Bush was challenged by Democratic Senator John Kerry of Massachusetts and his running mate North Carolina Senator John Edwards. At the heart of the debate was the decision of George Bush to invade Iraq. Bush told the country his reason for attacking Iraq was to look for:

> **a.** terrorists. **b.** terrorist training camps.
> **c.** Saddam Hussein. **d.** weapons of mass destruction.

★ ★ ★

235. TV attack ads were produced by independent political groups referred to as "527's (named for the tax code in which they are described) in an effort to influence the election. Which group sponsored ads attacking John Kerry's record in Vietnam?

> **a.** The Swift Boat Republicans **b.** The Swift Boat Veterans
> **c.** Republican Veterans for Bush **d.** The Independent Veterans

★ ★ ★

236. While many people felt that the major issues of the election were the economy, health care and the war on terror, approximately 22% of voters named this issue as being very important to them:

> **a.** Health care **b.** Education
> **c.** "Moral values" **d.** The environment

234. **d. weapons of mass destruction.** The United States had been faced with the worst terrorist attack in its history on September 11, 2001. The destruction of the World Trade Center in New York and the loss of close to 3,000 innocent lives awoke Americans to the danger of international terrorism. In October, 2001, the United States invaded Afghanistan, where terrorists were training, to set it on a path to free elections and democratic rule. George Bush then told the American people and Congress that he wanted to search for weapons of mass destruction in Iraq. After receiving authority from Congress, he sent American troops into Baghdad in March, 2003, and Iraqi leader Saddam Hussein was deposed and later captured. However, attacks by insurgents against U.S. forces destabilized the country, making a peaceful transition to a democratic form of government impossible. By the election, over 1,000 U.S. soldiers had lost their lives, along with thousands of Iraqi civilians. John Kerry charged that the Bush administration was handling the war in Iraq poorly and had no plan to control the ensuing insurgent attacks.

★ ★ ★

235. **b. The Swift Boat Veterans.** In spite of John Kerry's record as a decorated Vietnam veteran, a group known as the Swift Boat Veterans produced attack ads about his military service. At first, Kerry didn't respond to the ads, but later denounced them.

★ ★ ★

236. **c. "Moral values."** By election day the outcome was too close to call. Exit polls initially indicated a Kerry win, but the next day the electoral vote count was Bush: 286, Kerry: 252. When the Electoral College met in December, one Democratic elector from Minnesota voted for John Edwards, leaving Kerry with 251. Bush carried the South, the Central Plains states and part of the Midwest; Kerry, the Northeast, Upper Midwest and the West Coast. Although Bush won a record 62 million popular votes, John Kerry also received a record number of votes - 59 million.

PRESIDENTIAL CANDIDATES ★ 1789-2004

	CANDIDATE	PARTY	ELECTORAL VOTE
★1789★	George Washington		69
	John Adams		34
	John Jay		9
	Robert H. Harrison		6
	John Rutledge		6
	John Hancock		4
	George Clinton		3
	Samuel Huntington		2
	John Milton		2
	James Armstrong		1
	Benjamin Lincoln		1
	Edward Telfair		1
	Votes not cast		8
★1792★	George Washington	Federalist	132
	John Adams	Federalist	77
	George Clinton	Republican	50
	Thomas Jefferson	Republican	4
	Aaron Burr	Republican	1
	Votes not cast		6
★1796★	John Adams	Federalist	71
	Thomas Jefferson	Republican	68
	Thomas Pinckney	Federalist	59
	Aaron Burr	Republican	30
	Samuel Adams	Federalist	15
	Oliver Ellsworth	Federalist	11
	George Clinton	Republican	7
	John Jay	Federalist	5
	James Iredell	Federalist	3
	John Henry	Republican	2
	Samuel Johnston	Federalist	2
	George Washington	Federalist	2
	Charles Pinckney	Federalist	1
★1800★	Thomas Jefferson	Republican	73
	Aaron Burr	Republican	73
	John Adams	Federalist	65
	Thomas Pinckney	Federalist	64
	John Jay	Federalist	1

CANDIDATE	PARTY	POPULAR VOTE %	ELECTORAL VOTE
★1804★ Thomas Jefferson	Republican		162
Charles C. Pinckney	Federalist		14
★1808★ James Madison	Republican		122
Charles C. Pinckney	Federalist		47
George Clinton	Republican		6
not voted			1
★1812★ James Madison	Republican		128
DeWitt Clinton	Federalist		89
not voted			1
★1816★ James Monroe	Republican		183
Rufus King	Federalist		34
not voted			4
★1820★ James Monroe	Republican		231
John Quincy Adams	Republican		1
votes not cast			3
★1824★ Andrew Jackson	Republican	42%	99
John Quincy Adams	Republican	32%	84
William Crawford	Republican	13%	41
Henry Clay	Republican	13%	37
★1828★ Andrew Jackson	Democratic	56%	178
John Quincy Adams	Nat'l. Republican	44%	83
★1832★ Andrew Jackson	Democratic	55%	219
Henry Clay	Nat'l. Republican	42%	49
John Floyd	Indep. Democrat	2%	11
William Wirt	Anti-Masons	1%	7
votes not cast			2
★1836★ Martin van Buren	Democratic	51%	170
William Henry Harrison	Whig	36%	73
Hugh Lawson White	Whig	10%	26
Daniel Webster	Whig	3%	14
Willie Mangum	Indep. Democrat		11
★1840★ William Henry Harrison	Whig	53%	234
Martin van Buren	Democratic	47%	60
★1844★ James K. Polk	Democratic	50%	170
Henry Clay	Whig	48%	105
James G. Birney	Liberty	2%	0
★1848★ Zachary Taylor	Whig	47%	163
Lewis Cass	Democratic	43%	127
Martin van Buren	Free Soil	10%	0

| | | POPULAR | ELECTORAL |
CANDIDATE	PARTY	VOTE %	VOTE
★ 1852 ★ Franklin Pierce	Democratic	51%	254
Winfield Scott	Whig	44%	42
John P. Hale	Free Soil	5%	0
★ 1856 ★ James Buchanan	Democratic	45%	174
John C. Fremont	Republican	33%	114
Millard Fillmore	American	22%	8
★ 1860 ★ Abraham Lincoln	Republican	40%	180
John Breckenridge	Democratic	18%	72
John Bell	Const. Union	13%	39
Stephen Douglas	Democratic	29%	12
★ 1864 ★ Abraham Lincoln	Republican	55%	212
George McClellan	Democratic	45%	21
not voted			1
★ 1868 ★ Ulysses S. Grant	Republican	53%	214
Horatio Seymour	Democratic	47%	80
★ 1872 ★ Ulysses S. Grant	Republican	56%	286
Horace Greeley	Dem., Liberal Repub.	44%	

(Greeley died after the election; his 66 electoral votes were split among):

Thomas A. Hendricks	Dem., Liberal Repub.		42
B. Gratz Brown	Dem., Liberal Repub.		18
Charles Jenkins	Dem., Liberal Repub.		2
David Davis	Dem., Liberal Repub.		1
(for Greeley) not counted			3
★ 1876 ★ Rutherford B. Hayes	Republican	48%	185
Samuel Tilden	Democratic	51%	184
Peter Cooper	Greenback	1%	0
★ 1880 ★ James A. Garfield	Republican	48.3%	214
Winfield Scott Hancock	Democratic	48.2%	155
James B. Weaver	Greenback	3.2%	0
★ 1884 ★ Grover Cleveland	Democratic	49%	219
James G. Blaine	Republican	48%	182
Benjamin Butler	Greenback	2%	0
John St. John	Prohibition	1%	0
★ 1888 ★ Benjamin Harrison	Republican	48%	233
Grover Cleveland	Democratic	49%	168
Clinton Fisk	Prohibition	2%	0
Alson Streeter	Union Labor	1%	0

	CANDIDATE	PARTY	POPULAR VOTE %	ELECTORAL VOTE
★1892★	Grover Cleveland	Democratic	46%	277
	Benjamin Harrison	Republican	43%	145
	James B. Weaver	People's	9%	22
	John Bidwell	Prohibition	2%	0
★1896★	William McKinley	Republican	51%	271
	William Jennings Bryan	Democratic	47%	176
	John Palmer	Nat'l. Democratic	1%	0
	Joshua Levering	Prohibition	1%	0
★1900★	William McKinley	Republican	52%	292
	William Jennings Bryan	Democratic	46%	155
	Eugene Victor Debs	Social Democratic	.7%	0
★1904★	Theodore Roosevelt	Republican	56%	336
	Alton B. Parker	Democratic	38%	140
	Eugene Victor Debs	Socialist	3%	0
★1908★	William Howard Taft	Republican	52%	321
	William Jennings Bryan	Democratic	43%	162
	Eugene Victor Debs	Socialist	3%	0
★1912★	Woodrow Wilson	Democratic	42%	435
	Theodore Roosevelt	Bull Moose	27%	88
	William Howard Taft	Republican	23%	8
	Eugene Victor Debs	Socialist	6%	0
★1916★	Woodrow Wilson	Democratic	49%	277
	Charles Evans Hughes	Republican	46%	254
	A.L. Benson	Socialist	3%	0
★1920★	Warren G. Harding	Republican	61%	404
	James M. Cox	Democratic	35%	127
	Eugene Victor Debs	Socialist	3%	0
★1924★	Calvin Coolidge	Republican	54%	382
	John W. Davis	Democratic	29%	136
	Robert LaFollette	Progressive	17%	13
★1928★	Herbert Hoover	Republican	58%	444
	Alfred E. Smith	Democratic	41%	87
	Norman Thomas	Socialist	1%	0
★1932★	Franklin D. Roosevelt	Democratic	57%	472
	Herbert Hoover	Republican	40%	59
	Norman Thomas	Socialist	2%	0

		POPULAR	ELECTORAL
CANDIDATE	PARTY	VOTE %	VOTE
★ **1936** ★ Franklin D. Roosevelt	Democratic	61	523
Alf M. Landon	Republican	37%	8
Norman Thomas	Socialist	.4%	0
★ **1940** ★ Franklin D. Roosevelt	Democratic	55%	449
Wendell Willkie	Republican	45%	82
Norman Thomas	Socialist		0
★ **1944** ★ Franklin D. Roosevelt	Democratic	53%	432
Thomas E. Dewey	Republican	46%	99
Norman Thomas	Socialist	.2%	0
★ **1948** ★ Harry Truman	Democratic	49%	303
Thomas E. Dewey	Republican	45%	189
J. Strom Thurmond	States' Rights	2%	39
Henry A. Wallace	Progressive	2%	0
Norman Thomas	Socialist	.3%	0
★ **1952** ★ Dwight D. Eisenhower	Republican	55%	442
Adlai Stevenson	Democratic	44%	89
★ **1956** ★ Dwight D. Eisenhower	Republican	57%	457
Adlai Stevenson	Democratic	42%	73
Walter B. Jones	Independent		1
★ **1960** ★ John F. Kennedy	Democratic	49.7%	303
Richard M. Nixon	Republican	49.5%	219
Harry F. Byrd	Independent	.8%	15
★ **1964** ★ Lyndon Johnson	Democratic	61%	486
Barry Goldwater	Republican	39%	52
★ **1968** ★ Richard Nixon	Republican	43.4%	301
Hubert Humphrey	Democratic	42.7%	191
George Wallace	American Indep.	13.5%	46
★ **1972** ★ Richard Nixon	Republican	61%	520
George McGovern	Democratic	38%	17
John Hospers	Libertarian		1
★ **1976** ★ Jimmy Carter	Democratic	50%	297
Gerald Ford	Republican	48%	240
Ronald Reagan	Republican		1
Eugene McCarthy	Independent	1%	0
★ **1980** ★ Ronald Reagan	Republican	51%	489
Jimmy Carter	Democratic	41%	49
John Anderson	Independent	7%	0
★ **1984** ★ Ronald Reagan	Republican	59%	525
Walter Mondale	Democratic	41%	13

CANDIDATE	PARTY	POPULAR VOTE %	ELECTORAL VOTE
★1988★George H.W. Bush	Republican	54%	426
Michael Dukakis	Democratic	46%	111
Lloyd Bentsen	Democratic		1
★1992★Bill Clinton	Democratic	43%	370
George H.W. Bush	Republican	37%	168
H. Ross Perot	Independent	19%	0
★1996★Bill Clinton	Democratic	50%	379
Robert Dole	Republican	41%	159
H. Ross Perot	Reform Party	9%	0
★2000★George W. Bush	Republican	48%	271
Albert Gore	Democratic	49%	266
Ralph Nader	Green Party	3%	0
votes not cast			1
★2004★George W. Bush	Republican	51%	286
John Kerry	Democratic	48%	251
John Edwards	Democratic		1
Ralph Nader	Independent	1%	0

★THE PRESIDENTS OF THE UNITED STATES★

	YEARS SERVED	PARTY
1. George Washington, Va.	1789-1797	Federalist
2. John Adams, Ma.	1797-1801	Federalist
3. Thomas Jefferson, Va.	1801-1809	Republican
4. James Madison, Va.	1809-1817	Republican
5. James Monroe, Va.	1817-1825	Republican
6. John Quincy Adams, Ma.	1825-1829	Republican
7. Andrew Jackson, Tn.	1829-1837	Democratic
8. Martin van Buren, N.Y.	1837-1841	Democratic
9. William Henry Harrison, Oh.	1841	Whig
10. John Tyler, Va.	1841-1845	Whig
11. James K. Polk, Tn.	1845-1849	Democratic
12. Zachary Taylor, La.	1849-1850	Whig
13. Millard Fillmore, N.Y.	1850-1853	Whig
14. Franklin Pierce, N.H.	1853-1857	Democratic
15. James Buchanan, Pa.	1857-1861	Democratic
16. Abraham Lincoln, Il.	1861-1865	Republican
17. Andrew Johnson, Tn.	1865-1869	Democratic
18. Ulysses S. Grant, Il.	1869-1877	Republican
19. Rutherford B. Hayes, Oh.	1877-1881	Republican
20. James A. Garfield, Oh.	1881	Republican
21. Chester A. Arthur, N.Y.	1881-1885	Republican
22. Grover Cleveland, N.Y.	1885-1889	Democratic

★THE PRESIDENTS OF THE UNITED STATES★

	YEARS SERVED	PARTY
23. Benjamin Harrison, In.	1889-1893	Republican
24. Grover Cleveland, N.Y.	1893-1897	Democratic
25. William McKinley, Oh.	1897-1901	Republican
26. Theodore Roosevelt, N.Y.	1901-1909	Republican
27. William Howard Taft, Oh.	1909-1913	Republican
28. Woodrow Wilson, N.J.	1913-1921	Democratic
29. Warren G. Harding, Oh.	1921-1923	Republican
30. Calvin Coolidge, Ma.	1923-1929	Republican
31. Herbert Hoover, Ca.	1929-1933	Republican
32. Franklin D. Roosevelt, N.Y.	1933-1945	Democratic
33. Harry S Truman, Mo.	1945-1953	Democratic
34. Dwight D. Eisenhower, N.Y.	1953-1961	Republican
35. John F. Kennedy, Ma.	1961-1963	Democratic
36. Lyndon Johnson, Tx	1963-1969	Democratic
37. Richard Nixon, Ca.	1969-1974	Republican
38. Gerald Ford, Mi.	1974-1977	Republican
39. Jimmy Carter, Ga.	1977-1981	Democratic
40. Ronald Reagan, Ca.	1981-1989	Republican
41. George H. W. Bush, Tx.	1989-1993	Republican
42. Bill Clinton, Ar.	1993-2001	Democratic
43. George W. Bush, Tx.	2001-	Republican

NOTES

1. #3: *"The Electoral College"*, William C. Kimberling, http:// www.fec.gov/pdf/eleccoll.pdf(November, 2004).
2. #4: Kelly, Kate, *Election Day, An American Holiday, An American History,* (Facts on File, New York, 1991), 76.
3. #4: *"The Electoral College"*, Kimberling, *www.fec.gov.*
4. #7: *"Franklin Delano Roosevelt"*, http://geocities.com/presfacts/delanoroosevelt.html, 2004.
5. #14: *"New Hampshire's First in the Nation Primary"*, Hugh Gregg, *State of New Hampshire Manual for the General Court, (Department of State), No. 55, 1997,* http://politicallibrary.org/Timeline_files/Timeline2.htm,2004.
6. #15: http://en.wikipedia.org/wiki/Super_Tuesday, 2004.
7. #15:*"Presidential Elections"* Part III, Congressional Quarterly, 318
8. #32: Keysaar, Alexander, *The Right to Vote,* (Basic Books, New York, 2000), 143.
9. #33: *"Etymologies and Word Origins,"* Last updated 15 August 2004 © 1997-2004, by David Wilton. All rights reserved. http:/www.wordorigins.org/wordoro.htm
   Boller, Jr., Paul F., *Presidential Campaigns,* (Oxford University Press, 1996), 76-77, from: Allen Walker Read, "The Evidence on 'O.K.'," *Saturday Review of Literature,* XXIV (July19,1941), 3-10.
10. #35: Kelly, 159-60.
11. #37: *"Origin of 'GOP' "*, http://www.gop.com.
12. #39: Boller, 174, from Paolo Coletta, *William Jennings Bryan: Political Evangelist, 1860-1908* (Lincoln, Nebraska, 1965), 180; M.W. Werner, *William Jennings Bryan* (NewYork, 1929), 86; John A. Garraty, *Henry Cabot Lodge* (New York, 1953), 174.
13. #40: Boller, 108, from Melvin L. Hayes, *Mr. Lincoln Runs for President* (Citadel Press, New York, 1960), 120-21, Meade Minnegerode, *Presidential Years, 1789-1860 (*New York, 1928), 378
14. #46: *"Electoral College,"* Microsoft ® Online Encyclopedia 2004 http://encarta.msn.com © 1997-2004 Microsoft Corporation. All Rights Reserved.
15. #56: DeGregorio, Willam A., *The Complete Book of U.S. Presidents,* (Random House), 1993), 129.
16. #65: Kelly, 30.

17. **#66:** *"Chronology of Presidential Elections,"* Congressional Quarterly, Part III, 226.
18. **#67:** McPherson, James M., general editor, *To the Best of My Ability: The American Presidency,* Gordon S. Wood: *"Campaign of 1789",* (Dorling Kindersley, New York, 2001), 310.
19. **#68:** McPherson, Gordon S. Wood: *"Campaign of 1789",* 310.
20. **#72:** Boller, 8, from Minnegerode, *Presidential Years,* 65.
21. **#72:** Ibid., 8, from David Burner et al., *The American People,* (St. James, N.Y., 1980), 124.
22. **#77:** McPherson, Gordon S. Wood, *George Washington,* 20.
23. **#80:** Ibid., Richard M. Pious, *Campaign of 1800,* 316.
24. **#81:** Thompson, Peter, *Dictionary of American History from 1763 to the Present,* (Checkmark Books, 2000), 236.
25. **#84:** *Notes of Debates in the Federal Convention of 1787 reported by James Madison,* Adrienne Koch, ed., xii, from Gaillard Hunt, *The Writings of James Madison,* IX, (New York, 1900-10), G. P. Putnam's Sons, 533.
26. **#85:** DeGregorio, 50.
27. **#89:** Ibid., 63.
28. **#92:** Borneman, Walter R., *1812, The War That Forged A Nation,* (Harper Collins, New York, 2004), 240-41, 245, 248.
29. **#94:** Schlesinger, Arthur M. Jr., *History of American Presidential Elections, 1789-2001,* 11 Volumes, Lynn W. Turner, *Elections of 1816 and 1820, Excerpt from William Plumer Papers,* (Chelsea House Publishers, Philadelphia, 2002), Vol. 1, 342.
30. **#94:** Ibid., Lynn W. Turner, *"Election of 1820",* Vol. I, 342-43.
31. **#98:** Ibid., James F. Hopkins, *"Election of 1824",* Vol. I, 364
32. **#104:** Ibid., Robert V. Remini, *"Election of 1828",* Vol. II, 422.
33. **#105:** *"The American Whig Party",* Hal Morris, http://www.earlyrepublic.net/whigs.htm, 2004.
34. **#108:** Boller, 65-6, DeGregorio, 142.
35. **#112:** McPherson, Richard M. Pious, *Campaign of 1844,* 349.
36. **#114:** McPherson, Catherine Clinton, *Zachary Taylor,* 92.
37. **#115:** DeGregorio, 180-81.
38. **#116:** Ibid., 204.
39. **#118:** Ibid., 192.
40. **#119:** *"My Doughface Cousin",* John Morton Jones J. D., http:www.redlandsfortnightly.org/Jones03.htm, 2003.

41. #122: DeGregorio, 217.
42. #126: Ibid., 234.
43. #128: Boller, 118, from John G. Nicolay and John Hay, eds.,
  Complete Works of Abraham Lincoln, 13 vols., (Harrogate,
  Tenn., 1894), X:263-64.
44. #128: Ibid., 115, from *Works of Lincoln,*VIII:100-101.
45. #129: Ibid., 117, from Sandburg: *Abraham Lincoln: The War
  Years,* III:271.
46. #129: Boller, 117, from " 'Conservative' Ribaldry, "
  Harper'sWeekly, VIII (September 24, 1864), 610;
  Sandburg, *War Years,* III:389-90.
47. #130: Boller, 17, from Macartney, *McClellan*, 348; *Lincoln and the
  Civil War in the Diaries and Letters of John Hay,* ed.: Tyler
  Dennett, New York, 1939), 233.
48. #130: Boller, 118-19, from J.G. Randall, "The Unpopular Mr.
  Lincoln," *Abraham Lincoln Quarterly*, II (June 1943), 275.
49. #133: Thompson, 167.
50. #133: Boller, 125, from J.L. Ringwalt, *Anecdotes of Gen.Ulysses S.
  Grant* (Philadelphia,1886),69-70
51. #136: Schlesinger, William Gillette, *"Election of 1872"*, Vol. IV,
  1321.
52. #136: McPherson, Richard M.Pious, *Campaign of 1872,* 370.
53. #137: Boller, 131-32, from Ida Usted Harper, *Life and Work
  of Susan B. Anthony*, 2 vols. (Indianapolis, 1898), I:409-65:
  Rheta Childs Dorr, *Susan B. Anthony* (Garden City, N.Y.,
  1954), 273-304.
54. #143: Garraty, *The Story of America,* (Holt, Rinehart and Winston,
  1994), 704-05.
55. #144: Thompson, 402.
56. #145: *Webster's New Universal Unabridged Dictionary,* Second
  Deluxe Edition,(Simon and Schuster, New York, 1983),
  1179.
57. #146: DeGregorio, 322, 325-26, Boller, 148-49.
58. #147: McPherson, Richard M. Pious, *Campaign of 1888,* 380.
59. #147: Kelly, 158.
60. #147: Ibid., 158, from Samuel P. Orth, *The Boss and the
  Machine,* (Yale University Press, New Haven, 1919) 150.
61. #147: Ibid., 158, 159.
62. #148: William C. Kimberling, *The Electoral College,*
  http://www.fec.gov/pdf/eleccoll.pdf.
63. #151: Boller, 163.
64. #152: Ibid., 166.

65. #153: Schlesinger, Gilbert C. Fite, *"Election of 1896"*, Vol. V, 1788.

66. #153: Boller, 168, from M.W. Werner, *William Jennings Bryan*, (New York, 1929) p. 75-6, Paxton Hibben, *The Peerless Leader: William Jennings Bryan*, 187.

67. #156: Ibid., 180.

68. #157: DeGregorio, 362

69. #158: Boller, 182, from Cyrenus Cole, *I Remember, I Remember: A Book of Recollections* (Iowa City, Iowa, 1936), 293.

70. #158: Ibid., 182, from H. Wayne Morgan, *William McKinley and His America* (Syracuse University Press, Syracuse, N.Y., 1963), 508.

71. #159: DeGregorio, 385.

72. #160: Boller, 184, from John M. Blum, *The Republican Roosevelt* (Cambridge, Mass., 1954), 70.

73. #160: Morris, Edmund, *Theodore Rex*, (Random House, New York, 2001), 382.

74. #162: Douglas Linder © 2002 *The Scopes Trial: An Introduction*, Famous Trials in American History, http://www.law.umkc.edu/faculty/projects/ftrials/scopes/ evolut.htm (2004).

75. #165: DeGregorio, 416.

76. #167: Dalton, Kathleen, *Theodore Roosevelt, A Strenuous Life*, (Alfred A. Knopf, New York, 2002) 404.

77. #167: Boller, 195.

78. #167: DeGregorio, 388.

79. #168: McPherson, Richard M. Pious, *Campaign of 1916*, 403.

80. #168: Boller, 207.

81. #170: Garraty, *The Story of America*, 853.

82. #172: DeGregorio, 437.

83. #173: Thompson, 452-53.

84. #174: Boller, 220.

85. #175: DeGregorio, 454.

86. #176: Keysaar, 254-55.

87. #177: DeGregorio, 467.

88. #178: Ibid., 468.

89. #179: Thompson, 330-31.

90. #180: DeGregorio, 473-4.

91. #181: Zevin, Ben D., ed., *Nothing to Fear, The Selected Addresses of Franklin D. Roosevelt 1932-1945*, (Popular Library, New York, 1961), 16.

92. #183: Thompson, 276, 278, 28.

93. #185: McPherson, Richard M. Pious, *Campaign of 1936*, 418.

94. #186: DeGregorio, 491.

95. #188: McPherson, Richard M. Pious, *Campaign of 1940,* 420.

96. #188: Boller, 253.

97. #190: Ibid., 263.

98. #189: Kelly, 212, from the *St.-Louis-Post Dispatch,* November 7, 1944.

99. #190: Ibid., 262-63.

100. #196: DeGregorio, 586-7.

101. #197: Ibid., 538.

102. #197: Ibid., 534.

103. #199: Boller, 292, from Adlai E. Stevenson, *The New America* (New York, 1957), 3-14.

104. #200: Thompson, 240.

105. #202: DeGregorio, 553.

106. #203: Boller, 301, from Theodore C. Sorensen, *Kennedy* (Harper & Row Publishers, Inc., New York, 1965), 174.

107. #203: Boller, 304, from Sorensen, 180.

108. #204: Ibid., 308.

109. #206: Ibid., 310.

110. #206: DeGregorio, 571.

111. #206: Boller, 309.

112. #210: Ibid., 335.

113. #210: DeGregorio, 589.

114. #212: Ibid.: 595-96.

115. #214: Boller, 342, from Ruth C. Stapleton, *Brother Billy* (New York, 1978), 103.

116. #214: Ibid., 349.

117. #215: Ibid., 346.

118. #221: DeGregorio, 645.

119. #221: Ibid., 645-6.

120. #221: Boller, 370.

121. #223: DeGregorio, 689.

122. #225: Thompson, 313.

123. #231: www.infoplease.com/spot/campaign2000issues.html.

ABOUT THE AUTHOR

Marilyn Zupnik is a professional musician who has always had a great interest in American presidential history. She is a graduate of the Curtis Institute of Music in Philadelphia, where she studied the oboe. A native of Cleveland, she lives with her husband and son in Minneapolis.